1st EDITION

Perspectives on Diseases and Disorders

Speech Disorders

Mary E. Williams
Book Editor

PERSPECTIVES
On Diseases & Disorders

GALE
CENGAGE Learning·

Detroit • New York • San Francisco • New Haven, Conn • Waterville, Maine • London

Elizabeth Des Chenes, *Director, Publishing Solutions*

For more information, contact:
Greenhaven Press
27500 Drake Rd.
Farmington Hills, MI 48331-3535
Or you can visit our Internet site at gale.cengage.com

For product information and technology assistance, contact us at

Gale Customer Support, 1-800-877-4253
For permission to use material from this text or product, submit all requests online at www.cengage.com/permissions

Further permissions questions can be e-mailed to permissionrequest@cengage.com

Articles in Greenhaven Press anthologies are often edited for length to meet page requirements. In addition, original titles of these works are changed to clearly present the main thesis and to explicitly indicate the author's opinion. Every effort is made to ensure that Greenhaven Press accurately reflects the original intent of the authors. Every effort has been made to trace the owners of copyrighted material.

LIBRARY OF CONGRESS CATALOGING-IN-PUBLICATION DATA

Speech disorders / Mary E. Williams, book editor.
   p. cm. -- (Perspectives on diseases and disorders)
 Includes bibliographical references and index.
 ISBN 978-0-7377-5783-5 (hardcover)
 1. Speech disorders. 2. Speech therapy. 3. Stuttering. I. Williams, Mary E., 1960-
RC423.S63826 2012
616.85'5--dc23

2012005512

Printed in the United States of America
1 2 3 4 5 6 7 16 15 14 13 12

CONTENTS

Monique Laberge

Speech disorders might be characterized by problems with the way vocal sounds are formed, by an interruption in the flow of speech, or by voice pitch, intensity, or quality. Often, there is a combination of several different problems.

Larry Blaser

Articulate speech is unique to the human species. Its development is probably the result of evolutionary changes in the anatomy of the skull that emerged with the human ability to stand upright.

Nancy Lucker-Lazerson

Oral-motor speech disorders include apraxia, which is a difficulty in transmitting speech messages from the brain to the mouth. Lisps and difficulties with pronunciation are examples of articulation disorders. Phonological disorders occur when one has not learned the rules for how sounds work together to create words.

CHAPTER 3 Living with Speech Disorders

FOREWORD

"Medicine, to produce health, has to examine disease."
—Plutarch

Independent research on a health issue is often the first step to complement discussions with a physician. But locating accurate, well-organized, understandable medical information can be a challenge. A simple Internet search on terms such as "cancer" or "diabetes," for example, returns an intimidating number of results. Sifting through the results can be daunting, particularly when some of the information is inconsistent or even contradictory. The Greenhaven Press series Perspectives on Diseases and Disorders offers a solution to the often overwhelming nature of researching diseases and disorders.

From the clinical to the personal, titles in the Perspectives on Diseases and Disorders series provide students and other researchers with authoritative, accessible information in unique anthologies that include basic information about the disease or disorder, controversial aspects of diagnosis and treatment, and first-person accounts of those impacted by the disease. The result is a well-rounded combination of primary and secondary sources that, together, provide the reader with a better understanding of the disease or disorder.

Each volume in Perspectives on Diseases and Disorders explores a particular disease or disorder in detail. Material for each volume is carefully selected from a wide range of sources, including encyclopedias, journals, newspapers, nonfiction books, speeches, government documents, pamphlets, organization newsletters, and position papers. Articles in the first chapter provide an authoritative, up-to-date overview that covers symptoms, causes and effects, treatments, cures, and medical advances. The second chapter presents a substantial number of opposing viewpoints on controversial treatments and other current debates relating to the volume topic. The third chapter offers a variety of personal perspectives on the disease or disorder. Patients, doctors, caregivers, and loved ones represent just some of the voices found in this narrative chapter.

Each Perspectives on Diseases and Disorders volume also includes:

- An **annotated table of contents** that provides a brief summary of each article in the volume.

- An **introduction** specific to the volume topic.

- Full-color **charts and graphs** to illustrate key points, concepts, and theories.

- Full-color **photos** that show aspects of the disease or disorder and enhance textual material.

- **"Fast Facts"** that highlight pertinent additional statistics and surprising points.

- A **glossary** providing users with definitions of important terms.

- A **chronology** of important dates relating to the disease or disorder.

- An annotated list of **organizations to contact** for students and other readers seeking additional information.

- A **bibliography** of additional books and periodicals for further research.

- A detailed **subject index** that allows readers to quickly find the information they need.

Whether a student researching a disorder, a patient recently diagnosed with a disease, or an individual who simply wants to learn more about a particular disease or disorder, a reader who turns to Perspectives on Diseases and Disorders will find a wealth of information in each volume that offers not only basic information, but also vigorous debate from multiple perspectives.

INTRODUCTION

For much of the viewing public, the 2010 movie *The King's Speech* was an introduction to the world of speech disorders and the field of speech therapy. The film depicts the therapeutic partnership between the Duke of York—later King George VI—a British royal with a stuttering disorder, and Lionel Logue, the actor, dialogue coach, and speech therapist who had opened a London speech-correction clinic in 1924. While many other films have featured characters who stutter, *The King's Speech* was the first to focus on a main character undergoing treatment for stuttering and the first to be applauded for its realistic and nonstereotypical portrayal of a person who stutters.

Only a few details are known about Lionel Logue's techniques for treating stuttering, as he kept no clinical records, and his relationship with his clients remained confidential. Historians do know that Logue prescribed rigorous daily exercises for the king, including breathing exercises and vowel intonations, which can help relax the larynx and diaphragm and reduce the stress associated with speaking. Logue denounced the treatment that required speaking with pebbles in the mouth—a technique said to have been used by the Greek orator Demosthenes in the fourth century B.C.—and instead coached the king to substitute words, revise sentences, and pause before saying words that typically caused difficulty. Logue also helped the king rehearse for speeches by having him practice tongue twisters and read aloud at varying rates of speed. While King George was never "cured" of his stutter, he was able to speak more effectively and with less anxiety in certain situations. Logue's methods, in essence, helped the king to manage his stuttering and to communicate well in spite of it.

As successful as Logue may have been with King George, many speech-language pathologists today would take issue with some of his techniques and theories. Logue's belief that stuttering is caused by childhood trauma, for example, was later refuted by scientific research. Moreover, some speech therapists warn that the consistent practice of word substitution and sentence revision can become maladaptive behaviors for people who stutter, leading to even more anxiety and decreased self-esteem. Such differences of opinion have been an essential part of the development of the field of speech-language pathology. Indeed, experimentation, trial and error, and debates between various camps of speech and language scientists remain significant factors in the evolution of speech therapy.

The roots of speech-language pathology and speech therapy are found in the elocution movement of the nineteenth century. Many elocutionists—skilled orators, diction coaches, and speech teachers—set up practices to work with politicians, preachers, actors, singers, and others who wanted to improve their vocal performance. In 1872 telephone inventor and elocutionist Alexander Graham Bell opened the School of Vocal Physiology, offering classes for the deaf and for people with speech impediments. He used an approach developed by his father known as visible speech, a writing system that provided visual representations of the positions that the speech organs needed to be in to articulate different sounds. Bell was one among a number of prominent elocutionists who began to specialize in training people with certain communication disorders—typically the deaf or people who stuttered. By the dawn of the twentieth century, elocution, phonetics (the study and classification of speech sounds), and insights from brain research and the new science of psychology had converged to form the basis of the occupational field then known as "speech correction."

According to speech-language pathologist and historian Judy Duchan, the practice of speech correction evolved into the profession of speech therapy over four discrete periods in the twentieth century. First, during the formative years of 1900 to 1945, the field of speech therapy was increasingly seen as distinct from elocution and speech communication. Professionals began to set up clinics that incorporated medical and educational techniques for treating speech disorders. Therapies during this time often consisted of sensory and motor training, including instruction on the placement and use of articulators—the tongues, lips, and other organs of speech—for correct pronunciation. A typical treatment would consist of tongue exercises and repetitive practice drills. Duchan refers to these approaches as atomistic—beginning with small units of speech and building up to longer word sequences.

During the second stage of twentieth-century development, between 1945 and 1965, speech therapy shifted from a focus on the atomistic to the holistic. Practice drills would more often start with complete words rather than speech sounds. Clinicians had begun to recognize that speech was more than the physical pronunciation of words; speech was also an inner process involving symbol formation and linguistic processing. This shift in approach was due, in part, to the increased incidence of aphasia among soldiers injured during World War II. Aphasia is the partial or total loss of the ability to use or understand language, usually caused by stroke or trauma. Treating aphasics helped speech pathologists arrive at a fuller understanding of external speech as emerging from an internal mental process.

Between 1965 and 1975, the third developmental period, speech-language pathologists were increasingly influenced by behavioral psychology and by linguistics, the science of language. Language was seen as a structured system, and clinicians developed programs for teaching the rules of that system rather than focusing on how language was processed interiorly. Imitative drills

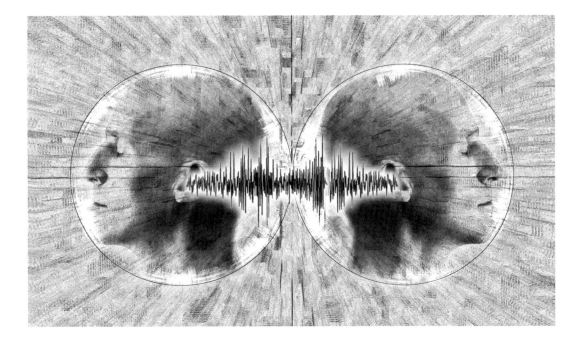

and positive reinforcement (verbal encouragement—and in some cases edible rewards) were frequently used with the intention of modifying the behavior of the person with the speech disorder.

Duchan refers to the fourth and current era of speech therapy, which began in 1975, as the pragmatics revolution. As the name suggests, today's clinicians focus more on the practical concerns of communication in everyday life, with an emphasis on social interaction and client-centered therapy. "Rather than conducting practice sessions in contexts separate from the client's ordinary communication situations, the clinical services [are] delivered in classrooms, homes, and in community settings,"[1] Duchan explains. The therapist tends to work collaboratively with clients, teachers, and family members to identify and achieve the life goals of the client.

Speech-language pathologists today are also more likely to be aware of the importance of therapeutic alliance (a sympathetic relationship between clinician and client) and

Speech disorders interrupt the flow of speech by affecting voice pitch, quality, intensity, or a combination of these. (© George Mattei/Photo Researchers, Inc.)

therapeutic allegiance (the shared belief that the treatment will be effective). This is where Lionel Logue, King George VI's speech therapist, may have been ahead of his time. In addition to exercises, practice drills, and speech coaching, Logue established and sustained a productive therapeutic relationship with his clients that addressed their motivation and sparked their desire for change. In her online history of Logue, speech-language pathologist Caroline Bowen writes:

> Why did Lionel Logue's methods work? From the little evidence we have I believe that his confidence, his empathy with his clients, and his understanding of the profoundly traumatic nature of a serious impediment to communication, combined with techniques to reduce inappropriate muscle tension and respiratory patterns, and to demonstrate to patients that there were many ways of producing fluent speech were all important.[2]

The world of speech-language pathology is, as this historical overview suggests, complex and broad. *Perspectives on Diseases and Disorders: Speech Disorders* provides an informative introduction to the struggles of living with and treating stuttering, apraxia, aphasia, and mutism. Many of those with conditions affecting expression and communication face feelings of shame, anxiety, and hopelessness. Through the perspectives of speech-language pathologists, scientific experts, and people who live with speech disorders, readers are invited to take a sympathetic look at this challenging family of disorders.

Notes

1. Judy Duchan, *A History of Speech-Language Pathology*, personal website, May 12, 2011. www.acsu.buffalo.edu /~duchan/new_history/overview.html.
2. Caroline Bowen, "Lionel Logue: Pioneer Speech Therapist," Speech-Language-Therapy.com, August 22, 2011. www.speech-language-therapy.com/ll.htm.

CHAPTER 1

Understanding Speech Disorders

Speech Disorders: An Overview

Monique Laberge

Speech disorders may manifest as an inability to produce intelligible or correctly enunciated words, as frequent breaks and interruptions to the flow of speech, or as problems affecting voice pitch and quality, explains Monique Laberge in the following overview. People with articulation disorders may omit sounds or substitute one sound for another, while those with phonological disorders often misinterpret the rules for how sounds are combined to produce words. Stutterers frequently repeat syllables and words, or struggle with an inability to articulate certain sounds. Other disorders, such as apraxia and dysarthria, may be caused by injury, brain damage, or impairment to the muscles involved in the production of speech, the author reports.

Speech-language pathologists have devised a variety of approaches to treating different speech disorders, including pronunciation training, sensory-motor awareness, articulation drills, relaxation strategies, breathing techniques, voice therapies, and orofacial exercises.

Laberge is a senior research investigator in the Department of Biochemistry and Biophysics at the University of Pennsylvania. As a science writer, she has contributed numerous articles to medical dictionaries and encyclopedias.

SOURCE: Monique Laberge, "Speech Disorders," *The Gale Encyclopedia of Nursing and Allied Health.* Belmont, CA: The Gale Group, 2006, p. 2513. Copyright © 2006 by The Gale Group. All rights reserved. Reproduced by permission.

Photo on previous page. Speech disorders are part of a broad category of disorders that also include language and hearing disorders. (© Sylwiaka/ Alamy)

A speech disorder is a communication disorder characterized by an impaired ability to produce speech sounds or normal voice, or to speak fluently. Speech disorders belong to a broad category of disorders called communication disorders that also include language and hearing disorders. Communication disorders affect one person out of every ten in the United States. Speech disorders refer to difficulties producing speech sounds or problems with voice quality. They may be characterized by an interruption in the flow or rhythm of speech such as stuttering, or by problems with the way sounds are formed, also called articulation or phonological disorders, or they may involve voice problems such as pitch, intensity, or quality. Often, there is a combination of several different problems.

Types of Speech Disorders

Speech disorders can either be present at birth or acquired as a result of stroke, head injury, or illness. The production of intelligible speech is the result of very complex interactions originating in the brain. When the brain sends a series of speech signals to the speech muscles, the muscles need to produce the series of sounds that will convey the intended message. Major speech disorders that can impair this process include:

- *Articulation disorders:* Articulation is the production of speech sounds, and persons affected by articulation disorders experience difficulty in being understood because they produce incorrect speech sounds. As a result, their speech is not intelligible. They may substitute one sound for another or may distort the sound with the result that it sounds incorrect, even though still recognizable, or omit one or more sounds in a word.
- *Phonological disorders:* Phonology is the science of speech sounds and sound patterns and of the language rules that dictate how sounds may be combined to

produce language. Persons affected by phonological disorders do not use the conventional rules for their native language but substitute their own variants. This affects classes of sounds, as opposed to single sounds. Sounds are characterized by where in the mouth they are produced, how they are produced, and by how the larynx (voice box) is used. Any unusual deviation in these features is called a phonological process. Fronting and backing are examples of phonological processes, characterized by the production of sounds at the front or at the back of the mouth when they should be produced the other way around. For example, the word "go," produced at the back of the mouth, might be used instead of "doe," which is produced in the front.

- *Stuttering:* Normal speech is fluent, in that it is spoken effortlessly and without hesitation. A break in fluent speech is called a dysfluency. Although some degree of dysfluency occurs in normal speech from time to time, stuttering has more dysfluencies than is considered average. Normally developing preschool children often demonstrate dysfluencies that are effortless and last for brief periods of time. However, changes in the types of dysfluency behavior and the frequency of occurrence may signal the development of a problem. Normal dysfluencies consist of word or sentence repetitions, fillers (um, ah), or interjections. Stuttering behavior includes sound or syllable repetition, prolongations (the unnatural stretching out of sounds), and blocks, which refers to an inability to produce the sound, as if it gets stuck and cannot come out. Stuttering dysfluencies are also often accompanied by tension and anxiety.

- *Voice disorders:* There are two types of voice disorders: organic voice and functional voice disorders. Organic voice disorders are associated with disease and require medical intervention. Functional voice disorders are the result of abuse or misuse of the larynx. Sounds are produced when the vocal cords of the throat come close together and vibrate with air coming from the lungs. These vibrations produce a series of pulses that then cause the air to resonate and produce voice sounds. People have unique voice characteristics and it is therefore difficult to define a normal voice. Generally speaking, a normal voice is pleasant sounding and has appropriate pitch and loudness for the age and gender of the speaker. A voice disorder is therefore present when the voice is not pleasant sounding, or when it is too loud or too soft or too high-pitched or low-pitched for the speaker's gender.

- *Apraxia:* This is a speech disorder in which voluntary muscle movement is impaired without muscle weakness. There are two main types of apraxias: buccofacial apraxia and verbal apraxia. Buccofacial apraxia impairs the ability to move the muscles of the mouth for non-speech purposes such as coughing, swallowing, and wiggling of the tongue. Verbal apraxia impairs the proper sequencing of speech sounds. Apraxias can either be acquired or developmental and have different degrees of severity, ranging from the inability to initiate speech to mild difficulties with the pronunciation of multi-syllabic words.

- *Dysarthria:* This is a speech disorder that affects the muscles involved in the production of speech. As a result, speech is slow, weak, inaccurate, and hesitant. The production of clear speech requires that several muscle systems work together. First, the lungs must provide the air required to activate speech. Then, the larynx must allow the air to vibrate. The soft palate that separates the oral and nasal cavities must also direct the air to one or both cavities to produce the different sounds. Finally, the lips, tongue, teeth, and jaw then must all move in a concerted way to shape the sounds into the various vowels, consonants, and syllables that make up the sounds of language. Dysarthria results from a weakness in any one of these elements or in the absence of proper coordination between them. If, for example, the lungs are weak, then speech will be too quiet or produced one word at a time. Childhood dysarthria can be present at birth or acquired as a result of disease or accident, as is the case for adult dysarthria.

Causes and Symptoms

The causes of articulation and phonological disorders are unclear, although it has been observed that they tend to develop in children before age four and run in families. The symptoms vary, depending on whether other disorders are present, but typically involve difficulty in making specific speech sounds. Articulation is considered a disorder when it is unintelligible or draws negative attention to the speaker. . . .

The causes of stuttering are not very well understood. There is some evidence that stuttering has a genetic cause since it has been observed to run in some families. According to the National Stuttering Association (NSA), current research suggests a connection between stuttering and the brain's ability to coordinate speech. The major symptom of stuttering, found in preschoolers but not adults, is persistent dysfluency of language that exceeds 10%.

The main causes of organic voice disorders include neuromuscular disorder, cancer, vocal cord paralysis, endocrine changes, various benign tumors such as inflammatory growths (granulomas), or consisting of a mass of blood vessels (hemangiomas) or occurring on mucous membranes (papillomas). Functional voice disorders are caused by abuse or misuse of the larynx. Misuse of the voice includes talking for excessively long periods of time or yelling. Abuse occurs as a result of excessive throat

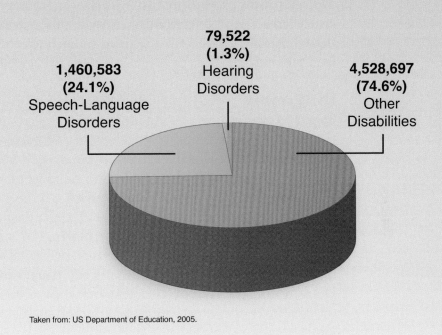

US Schoolchildren Receiving Services for Disabilities in 2005

1,460,583
(24.1%)
Speech-Language
Disorders

79,522
(1.3%)
Hearing
Disorders

4,528,697
(74.6%)
Other
Disabilities

Taken from: US Department of Education, 2005.

clearing, laughing, crying, coughing, or smoking. Both abuse and misuse of the voice can damage the vocal cords, or may result in nodules, polyps, contact ulcers, or edema.

Acquired apraxias occur as a result of brain damage and can often be linked to specific lesion sites on the brain. They can result from stroke, head injury, brain tumors, toxins, or infections. In the case of developmental apraxia of speech (DAS), it is usually present at birth. There are no specific lesion sites in the brain associated with DAS, and no direct cause has been identified. However, since young children only use a few words, it has been proposed that delays in language expression can impair a child's ability to gain control over the speech muscles.

Childhood dysarthria can be present at birth or acquired with diseases such as cerebral palsy, Duchenne muscular dystrophy, or myotonic dystrophy. Adult dysarthria may be caused by stroke, degenerative diseases such as Parkinson's or Huntington's disease, amyotrophic lateral sclerosis, multiple sclerosis, myasthenia gravis, meningitis, brain tumors, toxins, drug or alcohol abuse, or lead poisoning.

Diagnosis

Speech disorders are usually identified using a combination of hearing tests and physical exams. Physicians then recommend specialized evaluation by speech-language pathologists, who can best establish an accurate diagnosis.

A stuttering diagnosis is established on the basis of the type, frequency, and duration of speech dysfluency. The number of dysfluencies occurring in 100 words is counted to determine the dysfluency percentage. One half a stuttered word per minute is the usual criterion. Determining the type of stuttering behavior, either overt or covert, is the most important factor in diagnosing stuttering.

Organic and functional voice disorders are diagnosed with the assistance of an ear, nose, and throat specialist, an otolaryngologist, who can identify the organic cause of the voice disorder, if present. Several tests can be used to screen for possible tumors in the throat or laryngeal box area. Only in the absence of an organic cause will the voice disorder be diagnosed as functional, indicating that it is due to abuse or misuse of the voice.

A diagnosis of apraxia is not easy to establish but is usually indicated when children do not develop speech normally and are unable to produce consonant sounds.

Treatment

Speech pathologists have designed approaches for treating speech disorders with the type of treatment depending upon the type of impairment. A wide variety of treatment techniques are available for treating affected children, adolescents, and adults. A thorough assessment is normally conducted with the aim of determining the most effective and acceptable treatment approach for each disorder on an individual basis. A common treatment for many patients involves increasing sensory motor awareness of selected aspects of speech and systematically shaping the target speech behaviors.

Treatment for articulation/phonological disorders is usually based on increasing the affected person's awareness about how speech sounds make the meaning of words different. As a result, therapy often involves pronunciation exercises designed to teach how to produce sounds and words more clearly to increase understanding of the differences between the various speech sounds and words.

Treatment plans for stuttering depend on the severity of the dysfluency and may include seeing a speech-language pathologist. Most treatment plans include breathing techniques, relaxation strategies to help relax speech-associated muscles, posture control, and other exercises designed to help develop fluency.

FAST FACT

Between 6 million and 8 million Americans have a speech disorder.

Speech-language pathologists use many different approaches to treat voice problems. Functional voice disorders can often be successfully treated by voice therapy. Voice therapy involves identifying voice abuses and misuses and designing a course of treatment aimed at eliminating them. Voice disorders may require surgery if cancer is present.

Treatment of apraxia depends on the extent of the impairment. For individuals diagnosed with moderate to severe apraxia, therapy may be for them to start saying individual sounds and contrasting them, thinking about how the lips and tongue should be placed. Other specialized drills use the natural rhythm of speech to increase understanding. Individuals affected with mild apraxia are taught strategies to help them produce the words that

Stuttering is called a dysfluency. Stuttering behavior includes sound or syllable repetition, prolongations and blocks, and an inability to produce a sound. (© Ted Russell/Time Life Pictures/Getty Images)

give them difficulty. Several treatment programs have been developed for developmental apraxias. Some feature the use of touching cues, others modify traditional articulation therapies.

Treatment of dysarthria usually aims at maximizing the function of all speech systems with the use of compensatory strategies. Patients may be advised to take frequent pauses for breath, or to exaggerate articulation, or to pause before important words to emphasize them. If there is muscle weakness, orofacial exercises may also be prescribed to strengthen the muscles of the face and mouth that are used for speech. . . .

Prevention

Prevention of speech disorders is centered on identifying at-risk infants. The following conditions are considered to represent high-risk factors, and children exposed to them should be tested early and regularly:

- diagnosed medical conditions such as chronic ear infections
- biological factors such as fetal alcohol syndrome
- genetic defects such as Down syndrome
- neurological defects such as cerebral palsy
- family history such as family incidence of literacy difficulties

Stuttering can be prevented by parents avoiding undue corrections of dysfluency in their children. As young children begin to speak, some dysfluency is normal because they have a limited vocabulary and have difficulty expressing themselves. This results in dysfluent speech, and if parents place excessive attention on the dysfluency, a pattern of stuttering may develop. Speech therapy with children at risk for stuttering may prevent the development of a stuttering speech disorder.

The Evolution and Physiology of Speech

Larry Blaser

Animals may produce sounds to engage in a kind of rudimentary communication, but speech is unique to the human species, notes Larry Blaser in the following selection. With speech, humans are able to express complex ideas through sounds representing words with meanings. The development of speech probably resulted from evolutionary changes in human skull anatomy that emerged with the ability to stand upright, the author points out. These changes led to a larger brain, which enabled the development of a sophisticated speech and auditory center, as well as a more deeply placed larynx, which creates low vocal tones. Other elements of human physiology, including the diaphragm, thorax, jaw, palate, tongue, and teeth all work through coordination by the speech center of the brain to produce spoken language. Speech impediments are frequently the result of damage to the brain's speech center or abnormalities in the organs responsible for making words.

Blaser is a science writer who has contributed articles to encyclopedias and online digital science libraries.

SOURCE: Larry Blaser, "Speech," *The Gale Encyclopedia of Science.* Belmont, CA: The Gale Group, 2008, pp. 4066–4068. Copyright © 2008 by The Gale Group. All rights reserved. Reproduced by permission.

Speech is defined as the ability to convey thoughts, ideas, or other information by means of articulating sound into meaningful words.

Many animals can make sounds and some can tailor these sounds to a given occasion. They may sound an alarm that a predator is in the area, warning others of their species that something has trespassed into their territory. Animals may make soothing sounds to let offspring know that their parent is present. These are only sounds of varying pitch or volume and do not constitute speech. Some animals, notably birds, can copy human speech to a minor extent and repeat words that they have been taught. This may be speech but limited control of vocal cords and a lack of flexible lips restricts the sounds that birds can imitate.

Some great apes such as the gorilla have been taught speech via sign language. They do not have the ability to form words because their larynx is not constructed to allow them to form certain sounds necessary for human speech. Some researchers have worked diligently to teach an ape to sign with its hands, to point to symbols in a board, or arrange marked blocks to form a thought, however incomplete. Thus, a gorilla can indicate that he or she wants an orange, wants to rest, or is cold but cannot communicate outside of these limited signs. A gorilla certainly cannot speak. One chimpanzee learned to sign more than 100 words and to put two or three symbols together to ask for something, but she was never able to place symbols together to express an idea.

Speech is unique to the human species. It is a means by which a people's history can be handed down from one generation to the next. It enables one person to convey knowledge to a roomful of other people. It can be used to amuse, to rouse, to anger, to express sadness, to communicate needs that arise between two or more humans.

Theories on the Evolution of Speech

How have humans evolved to have the ability to talk while our close cousins, the great apes, have not? No definite answer can be given to that question though theories have been put forth.

One widely accepted theory has to do with the human's assumption of an erect (standing) position and the change that this brought to the anatomy of the skull. Following the evolution of human skulls from their earliest ancestors, one major change that occured is the movement of the foramen magnum (the large hole in the skull through which the spinal cord passes) to connect with the base of the brain. In early skulls, the foramen magnum is at the back of the skull because early man walked bent over with his head held to look straight ahead. The spinal cord entered the skull from behind as it does in apes and other animals. In modern humans, the opening

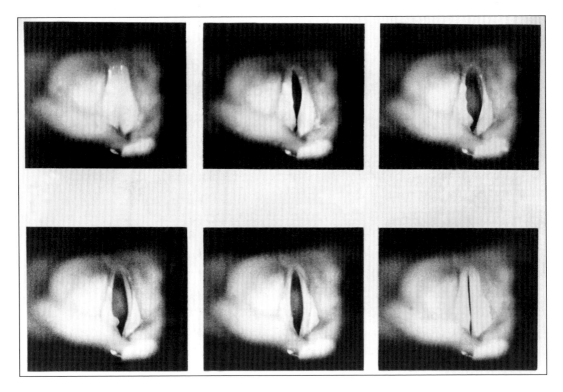

A multiple view of vocal cords at different points of vibration in speech. A series of muscles in and around the larynx pulls the vocal cords taut when speech is required.
(© Science Source/Photo Researchers, Inc.)

is on the bottom of the skull, reflecting humans' erect walk and his or her's skull placement atop the spine.

As humans' position changed and the manner in which his or her skull balanced on the spinal column pivoted, the brain expanded, altering the shape of the cranium. The most important change wrought by humans' upright stance is the position of the larynx in relation to the back of the oral cavity. As man became erect, his larynx moved deeper into the throat and farther away from the soft palate at the back of the mouth. This opened a longer resonating cavity that is responsible for the low vocal tones that man is capable of sounding.

The expanded brain allowed the development of the speech center where words could be stored and recalled. A more sophisticated auditory center provided the means by which speech by others of the same species could be recognized. Over time, and with greater control of the articulating surfaces, consonant sounds were added to the vocabulary. Initial sounds by hominids probably were vowels, as evidenced by current ape communication.

The Physiology of Speech

Speech requires movement of sound waves through the air. Speech itself is air that is moved from the lungs through a series of anatomic structures that mold sound waves into intelligible speech. This capacity can be accomplished in any volume from a soft whisper to a loud shout by varying the force and volume of air expelled from the lungs. All languages are spoken by the same mechanism, though the words are different and require different usages of the anatomy.

To expel air from the lungs the diaphragm at the floor of the thorax is relaxed. This allows the diaphragm to return to its resting position which is domed into the thorax, expelling air from the lungs. Also, the muscles of the chest tighten, reducing the size of the interior thorax to push more air from the lungs. The air travels up the windpipe (trachea) and passes through the larynx.

The larynx is comprised of a number of cartilages. The largest is the cricoid cartilage, which is joined to the top of the trachea. It is structurally different from the rings that form the trachea. The cricoid is a complete cartilaginous ring, while the tracheal rings are horse shoe shaped (open in the back). The back of the cricoid is a large, solid plate. The front slopes down sharply and forms a V angle. Atop the cricoid lies the thyroid cartilage, which is more elongated front to back in males. The cartilage forms an angle of about 90° in males. In females the cartilage is flatter, forming an angle of 120°. Thus the male cartilage protrudes farther forward and often is evident as a knob in front of the throat (known as the Adam's apple).

The two cartilages form a hard cartilagineous box that initiates sound by means of the vocal cords that lie at the upper end of the box. The glottis, entrance to the larynx at the upper end, is protected by a flap called the epiglottis. The flap is open during the process of breathing but closes over the glottis when food is swallowed. Both air and food traverse the same area in the throat, the pharynx, and the epiglottis prevents food from entering the trachea and directs air into the lungs. Infection of the epiglottis can occur when a child has a sore throat. The resulting inflammation can progress rapidly, cause complications in respiration, and may be fatal if not treated promptly because the inflamed epiglottis can close off the laryngeal opening.

Vocal Cords and Voice

If an individual is simply breathing and not talking, the vocal cords lie relaxed and open to allow free passage of air. A series of muscles in and around the larynx pulls the vocal cords taut when speech is required. The degree of stress on the cords dictates the tone of voice. Singing requires especially fine control of the laryngeal mechanism.

Word emphasis and emotional stress originate here. Air puffs moving through the larynx place the vocal cords or vocal folds in a state of complex vibration. Starting from a closed configuration the vocal folds open first at the bottom. The opening progresses upward toward the top of the fold. Before the opening reaches the top of the vocal cord the bottom has closed again. Thus the folds are open at the bottom and middle, open at the middle and closed on each end, open at the middle and top, and then only at the top. This sequence is repeated in fine detail during speech.

Once the sound leaves the vocal cords it is shaped into words by other structures called articulators. These are the movable structures such as the tongue and lips that can be configured to form a given sound.

> **FAST FACT**
>
> During a child's first three years, the brain is developing and maturing. This is the most intensive period for acquiring speech and language skills.

Tailoring Sounds into Words

Above the larynx lies the pharynx through which the sound moves on its way to the mouth. The mouth is the final mechanism by which sound is tailored into words. The soft palate at the back of the mouth, the hard or bony palate in the front, the teeth, the tongue, and the lips come into play during speech. The nose also provides an alternate means of issuing sound and is part of the production of speech. Movement of the entire lower jaw can alter the size of the mouth cavern and influence the tone and volume of the speech. Speech is a complex series of events that takes place with little or no conscious control from the speaker other than selection of the words to be spoken and the tone and volume at which to deliver them. The speech center in the brain coordinates movement of the anatomic structures to make the selected words become reality. Speaking in louder tones is accomplished by greater force on the air expelled from the lungs. Normal speech is accompanied by normal levels of respiration.

Whispering involves a reduction in the air volume passing through the vocal cords.

The tongue is the most agile of these articulators. Its musculature allows it to assume a number of configurations—flat, convex, curled, etc.—and to move front and back to contact the palate, teeth, or gums. The front of the tongue may move upward to contact the hard palate while the back of the tongue is depressed. Essentially these movements open or obstruct the passage of air through the mouth. During speech, the tongue moves rapidly and changes shapes constantly to form partial or complete occlusions of the vocal tract necessary to manufacture words. The vocal tract is open for formation of the vowels, moderately open to produce the R or L sounds, tightly constricted to S or F, and completely occluded for P and G.

In addition to the formation of words, speech entails rhythm. This rhythm can be seen by the motions made by the speaker as he or she talks. He or she may chop his or her hand or move his or her head in time to the stresses of speech, marking its rhythm. Rhythm is essentially the grouping of words and sounds in a time period. Rhythm often is most emphatic in children's taunts: "Thom-as is a teach-er's pet." In more complex speech the rhythm is not as exact but listeners are disposed to placing a rhythmic pattern on what they hear even though the speaker may not stress any such rhythm.

The Brain

The speech center lies in the parietal lobe of the left hemisphere of the brain for right-handed persons and most left-handed. The area of the brain responsible for motor control of the anatomic structures is called Broca's motor speech area. It is named for Pierre Paul Broca (1824–80) a French anatomist and surgeon who carried out extensive studies on the brain. The motor nerves leading to the neck and face control movements of the tongue, lips, and jaws.

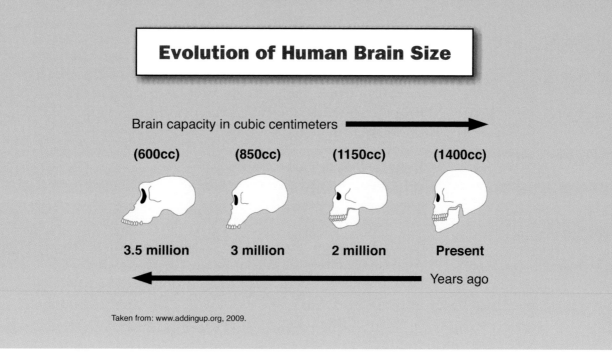

Evolution of Human Brain Size

Brain capacity in cubic centimeters ⟶

(600cc)   (850cc)   (1150cc)   (1400cc)

3.5 million   3 million   2 million   Present

⟵ Years ago

Taken from: www.addingup.org, 2009.

The language recognition center usually is situated in the right hemisphere. Thus a person who loses the capacity for speech still may be able to understand what is spoken to him or her and vice versa. The loss of the power of speech or the ability to understand speech or the written word is called aphasia.

Three speech disorders—dysarthria, dysphonia, and aphasia—result from damage to the speech center. Dysarthria is a defect in the articulation and rhythm of speech because of weakness in the muscles that form words. Amyotrophic lateral sclerosis ([ALS, or] Lou Gehrig's disease) and myasthenia gravis are two diseases with which such muscle weakness can be associated. Dysphonia is a hoarseness of the voice that can be caused by a brain tumor or any number of nonneurologic factors. Aphasia can be either motor aphasia, which is the inability to express thoughts in speech or writing, or sensory aphasia, the inability to read or to understand speech.

The ability to speak is inherent in the human species. . . . Language is passed from one generation to the next. Children learn basic language easily and at a young age.

From that time they add to their vocabulary as they accrue education and experience. A child will learn a language with the regional inflections inherent in his parents' and peers' speech.

Speech Impediments

Speech can be negatively influenced by abnormalities in the structures responsible for making words. Thickening of the vocal cords or tumor growth on the vocal cords can deepen the tone of speech. A cleft palate, a congenital anomaly, can be a serious impediment of speech. A cleft lip with the palate intact is a lesser problem, but may still interfere with the proper formation of words. Fortunately, surgical correction of either of these impediments is easily carried out.

Traumatic changes that cause loss of part of the tongue or interfere in the movement of the jaw also can result in speech changes. Extended speech therapy can help to make up for the loss in articulation.

A stroke can interfere with the function of the speech center or cause of motor control over the muscles used in speech because it destroys the part of the brain controlling nerves to those structures. Destruction of the speech center can render an individual unable to form meaningful sentences or words. Once destroyed, brain tissue is not regenerated. Loss of the speech center may mean a life without the ability to talk. In this case, the patient may need to rely solely on the written word. Recognition of speech and language is centered in a part of [the] brain apart from the speech center so a patient still could recognize what was said to him or her.

Distinguishing Oral-Motor, Articulation, and Phonological Disorders

Nancy Lucker-Lazerson

Nancy Lucker-Lazerson is a licensed speech-language patholo-gist practicing in Carlsbad, California. In the following article she defines and examines the differences between three broad catego-ries of speech impairments seen in children: oral-motor disorders, articulation disorders, and phonological disorders. Oral-motor disor-ders include childhood apraxia of speech, a difficulty in transmitting speech messages from the brain to the mouth, and dysarthria, a weakness of the lips, tongue, or jaw that interferes with speech. Typical articulation disorders include lisps and mispronunciations in which a child substitutes one sound for another. Phonological disorders, which may lead to reading and learning disabilities, occur when an individual does not grasp how sounds combine to make words. In most cases, Lucker-Lazerson asserts, children with speech-production disorders respond well to early and intensive therapy.

Your two-year-old says no words, makes some sounds, yet he understands everything you say. Your five-year-old speaks in what appear to be sentences, but all you hear are vowel sounds. Your seven-year-old lisps, and says "wabbit" instead of "rabbit". And your three-year-old talks non-stop, but no one can understand a word that he says. So what do you do? If you bring your child to a speech-language pathologist (SLP), the first two children would probably be diagnosed as having oral-motor planning deficits, or Childhood Apraxia of Speech (CAS). The third child has an Articulation disorder, and the fourth child has a Phonology disorder. Now that you know that, what does it all mean?

Oral-Motor Speech Disorders

Childhood Apraxia of Speech is a deficit in the ability to plan the motor movements for speech and is considered an oral motor planning disorder. Children with CAS have difficulties transmitting the speech message from their brain to their mouths. Children with significant weakness of the lips, tongue, and jaw may be diagnosed by a neurologist as having Dysarthria. Many children with cerebral palsy and multiple sclerosis have Dysarthria. CAS is usually of unknown origin. Whether or not we know the cause, SLPs can treat the disorder.

Oral-motor disorders are diagnosed by the SLP directly observing the child and completing an examination of both the child's speech and oral mechanism. The oral mechanism exam involves the SLP asking the child to do a variety of tasks (such as pursing lips, blowing, licking lips, elevating tongue, etc.), looks inside the child's mouth, observes the child eating, and listens to the child talk. The therapist will also listen for the child's ability to produce rapid oral movements. A diagnosis of CAS involves consonant and vowel distortions, distorted sound substitutions, errors consistent in type and place, and prosodic errors (prosody refers to pitch, rate, and rhythmic features of speech). Some other behaviors seen in CAS include groping, perseverative errors, and increasing errors as the length of utterance increases. The SLP will determine how "intelligible" the child is (how much of what the child says can other people understand?), and may complete a formal test (like the Kaufman Speech Praxis Test). Like a detective, a good diagnostician looks at many variables before making a diagnosis.

> **FAST FACT**
>
> Between 30 and 60 percent of children with a speech-language deficit have a sibling or a parent who is also affected, reports the American Speech-Language-Hearing Association.

For children who have CAS, therapy should address the movement patterns in syllables, progressing from the simple (one-syllable words with similar sounds at the beginning and end, like "pop," "mom," and "cake") to the complex (multi-syllabic words with many different sounds). There may also be a need to teach more functional responses (e.g. *yes, no, I want, I dont want, I need,* etc.). In more severe cases of CAS, a child may require an alternative/augmentative form of communication, such as sign language, a communication board, or an AAC (Augmentative/Alternative Communication) device. These are not intended to replace oral speech, but in fact, to facilitate it and to provide the child with a means of communicating with others. Therapy also needs to address prosody. Frequent drill and repetition is required for therapy to be successful. Intense, individual therapy is ideal for CAS. Group therapy is not recommended for CAS, and children with moderate to more severe deficits will require therapy for a number of years.

Articulation Disorders

When a child has a simple lisp (producing [th] instead of [s], like "thing" instead of "sing" or "yeth" instead of "yes"), substitutes [w] for [l] or [r], or other similar errors, they are demonstrating an articulation disorder. Articulation refers to the manner in which a child produces a sound and the placement of the tongue, lips, and teeth. Common articulation errors are those listed above, in addition to [f] for [th] ("fum" for "thumb"), [l] for [y] ("lelo" for "yellow"). Traditional thinking has been that some articulation errors are developmental in nature (e.g. s, l, r) and that children may not be ready to address them in therapy until a specific age (typically 7 or 8). However, current research has disproved the idea of developmental norms for articulation, and in fact, current best practice involves starting treatment with the more difficult sounds. In addition, the earlier therapy begins, the more successful it will be. Articulation errors may not significantly reduce the child's ability to be understood.

Articulation therapy consists of drill exercises and various cues to help the child correct their sound productions. These cues may be verbal (e.g. tell the child where to place his tongue) or visual (having the child look at the therapist's mouth or in a mirror) or tactile (i.e. touch; e.g. having the child slide their finger down their arm when making the [s] sound). Frequent practice is essential for articulation therapy to be successful.

Phonological Disorders

Phonology is the sound system of language. The phonology of language tells us how sounds fit together in words. Children who have phonology disorders have not learned the rules for how sounds fit together to make words, and use certain processes to simplify words. Phonology disorders are related to language and reading and are now seen as a language-based disorder. Children with phonology disorders are frequently unintelligible; often, their parents are the only ones who can understand them, and even they have difficulties. Children with these disorders are at a very high risk for later reading and learning disabilities, and should be treated with intensive speech therapy as soon as they are diagnosed, as early as age 3.

Typical Speech Development

Age	Speech Development
Birth–3 Months	• makes cooing and gooing sounds • cries differently for different needs • smiles at caregivers
4–6 Months	• babbling sounds more speech-like, with p, b, and m sounds • gurgles, chuckles, and laughs • vocalizes excitement and displeasure
7 Months–1 Year	• babbling, has both long and short groups of sounds, such as "tata upup bibibi" • uses non-crying sounds to get and keep attention • has one or two words (hi, dog, mama) around first birthday
1–2 Years	• says more words every month • puts two words together ("what's that?" "more cookie") • uses many different consonant sounds at the beginning of words
2–3 Years	• uses two or three words to talk about and ask for things • uses k, g, f, t, d, and n sounds • directs attention to objects by naming them
3–4 Years	• talks about activities at school or at friends' homes • sentences often have four or more words • usually talks easily without repeating syllables or words
4–5 Years	• sentences have lots of details ("the biggest peach is mine") • tells stories that stick to topic • says most sounds correctly except l, r, v, s, z, ch, sh, th • communicates easily with other children and adults

Taken from: American Speech-Language-Hearing Association. www.asha.org/public/speech/development.

A phonology disorder is most commonly diagnosed using the Assessment of Phonological Processes by Barbara Hodson. This test analyzes (by hand, or through a computer program) the patterns that a child is producing as they say 50 words. A phonological analysis can also be completed informally. There are other tests for phonology available, but the Hodson is the most widely used.

There are many different phonological processes which SLP's see and treat. One of the most common is called "cluster reduction". Children who use this process will take a sound blend (like [bl] [sp] or [tr]) and omit one of the sounds: "blue" becomes "boo", "spoon" becomes "poon", and "tree" becomes "ti". Another common process is called "velar fronting". Children who use this pro-

Children with childhood apraxia of speech have difficulties transmitting the speech message from their brain to their mouth. (© **Hattie Young/ Photo Researchers, Inc.**)

cess substitute sounds produced in the front of the mouth (t, d, n) for sounds produced in the back of the throat (k, g). In this instance, "duck" becomes "guk", "car" becomes "tar", "go" becomes "do" and "can" becomes "tan".

Therapy for phonological processes involves making the child more aware of the correct sound patterns (rules) and drilling the new patterns. Awareness is frequently achieved through what is referred to as "auditory bombardment"; using an amplifier and headphones, the therapist will repeatedly say words using the correct patterns. One popular therapy technique for remediating phonology disorders is called "cycling", developed by Barbara Hodson. In this approach, auditory bombardment is used, and children work on a specific process for a period of time, then move onto the next process, and so on. Once through all of the processes that need remediating, the cycles are repeated again and again. Another very effective technique is called "minimal pairs". In this technique, the therapist will present a pair of words to the child that addresses the incorrect sound pattern and enables the child to first discriminate, and later produce, the differences between sound patterns; e.g. if the child is omitting sounds in blends, a pair might be "Kate"/"skate" or "cool"/"school". If velar fronting is the problem, then a pair of words might be "tar"/"car" or "tan"/"can". A good therapist will use a variety of techniques in order to maximize therapy time.

The most important thing to remember about speech production disorders is that therapy can, in most cases, make a huge difference. The earlier and more intensive the intervention, the more successful the therapy. Group therapy can be effective for articulation disorders and some phonology disorders, but children with CAS really need the intensive, individual therapy.

The Impact of Stuttering

American Speech-Language-Hearing Association

Stuttering is a disorder in which repeated or prolonged sounds and interjections frequently disrupt the flow of speech, notes the American Speech-Language-Hearing Association (ASHA) in the following viewpoint. ASHA reports the following regarding the disorder: People who stutter may struggle for several moments to produce a word, sometimes becoming "blocked" in their speech. The disorder can impact one's daily life; people who stutter may restrict their activities, attempt to hide their disorder by rearranging the words in their sentences, or decline to speak. In diagnosing a person who stutters, speech-language pathologists evaluate them through tests, observations, and interviews to determine the extent of the impairment. Treatment for stuttering usually involves behavioral approaches that teach people to slow down their speech and practice with short sentences as they gradually increase fluency.

Those who interact with people who stutter should avoid interrupting them, completing their sentences, or appearing annoyed and impatient, according to ASHA. People who stutter communicate more smoothly when they are given the time to say what they need to say.

ASHA is a professional alliance of audiologists, speech-language pathologists, and speech, language, and hearing scientists.

*S*tuttering affects the fluency of speech. It begins during childhood and, in some cases, lasts throughout life. The disorder is characterized by disruptions in the production of speech sounds, also called "disfluencies." Most people produce brief disfluencies from time to time. For instance, some words are repeated and others are preceded by "um" or "uh." Disfluencies are not necessarily a problem; however, they can impede communication when a person produces too many of them.

In most cases, stuttering has an impact on at least some daily activities. The specific activities that a person finds challenging to perform vary across individuals. For some people, communication difficulties only happen during specific activities, for example, talking on the telephone or talking before large groups. For most others, however, communication difficulties occur across a number of activities at home, school, or work. Some people may limit their participation in certain activities. Such "participation restrictions" often occur because the person is concerned about how others might react to disfluent speech. Other people may try to hide their disfluent speech from others by rearranging the words in their sentence (circumlocution), pretending to forget what they wanted to say, or declining to speak. Other people may find that they are excluded from participating in certain activities because of stuttering. Clearly, the impact of stuttering on daily life can be affected by how the person and others react to the disorder.

Signs and Symptoms of Stuttering

Stuttered speech often includes *repetitions* of words or parts of words, as well as *prolongations* of speech sounds. These disfluencies occur more often in persons who stutter than they do in the general population. Some people who stutter appear very tense or "out of breath" when talking. Speech may become completely stopped or *blocked*. Blocked is when the mouth is positioned to say a sound, sometimes for several seconds, with little or no sound forthcoming. After some effort, the person may complete the word. Interjections such as "um" or "like" can occur, as well, particularly when they contain repeated ("u- um- um") or prolonged ("uuuum") speech sounds or when they are used intentionally to delay the initiation of a word the speaker expects to "get stuck on."

Some examples of stuttering include:

- *"W W W* Where are you going?" (Part-word repetition: The person is having difficulty moving from the "w" in "where" to the remaining sounds in the word. On the fourth attempt, he successfully completes the word.)
- *"SSSS* ave me a seat." (Sound prolongation: The person is having difficulty moving from the "s" in "save" to the remaining sounds in the word. He continues to say the "s" sound until he is able to complete the word.)
- "I'll meet you—*um um you know like*—around six o'clock." (A series of interjections: The person expects to have difficulty smoothly joining the word "you" with the word "around." In response to the anticipated difficulty, he produces several interjections until he is able to say the word "around" smoothly.)

How Is Stuttering Diagnosed?

Identifying stuttering in an individual's speech would seem like an easy task. Disfluencies often "stand out" and disrupt a person's communication. Listeners can usually detect when a person is stuttering. At the same time, however, stuttering can affect more than just a person's observable speech. Some characteristics of stuttered speech are not as easy for listeners to detect. As a result, diagnosing stuttering requires the skills of a certified speech-language pathologist (SLP).

During an evaluation, an SLP will note the number and types of speech disfluencies a person produces in various situations. The SLP will also assess the ways in which the person reacts to and copes with disfluencies. The SLP may also gather information about factors such as teasing that may make the problem worse. A variety of other assessments (e.g., speech rate, language skills) may be completed as well, depending upon the person's age and history. Information about the person is then analyzed to determine whether a fluency disorder exists. If so, the extent to which it affects the ability to perform and participate in daily activities is determined.

During an evaluation for speech disorders a speech-language pathologist notes the number of speech disfluencies a person produces in various situations and then assesses the way the person reacts to and copes with the disfluencies. (© Christina Kennedy/Alamy)

Risk Factors for Children

For young children, it is important to predict whether the stuttering is likely to continue. An evaluation consists of a series of tests, observations, and interviews designed

Childhood Stuttering and Gender

The ratio of boys to girls who persist in stuttering is three to one.

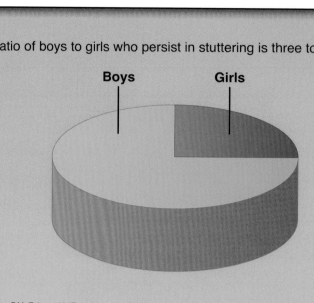

Taken from: P.M. Zebrowski. "Developmental Stuttering." *Pediatric Annals* 32(7):453-458. July 2003.

to estimate the child's risk for continuing to stutter. Although there is some disagreement among SLPs about which risk factors are most important to consider, factors that are noted by many specialists include the following:

- a family history of stuttering
- stuttering that has continued for 6 months or longer
- presence of other speech or language disorders
- strong fears or concerns about stuttering on the part of the child or the family

No single factor can be used to predict whether a child will continue to stutter. The combination of these factors can help SLPs determine whether treatment is indicated.

Evaluating Older Children

For older children and adults, the question of whether stuttering is likely to continue is somewhat less important, because the stuttering has continued at least long enough for it to become a problem in the person's daily life. For these individuals, an evaluation consists of tests, observations, and interviews that are designed to assess the overall severity of the disorder. In addition, the impact the disorder has on the person's ability to communicate and participate appropriately in daily activities is evaluated. Information from the evaluation is then used to develop a specific treatment program, one that is designed to:

- help the individual speak more fluently,
- communicate more effectively, and
- participate more fully in life activities.

Treatments for Stuttering

Most treatment programs for people who stutter are "behavioral." They are designed to teach the person specific skills or behaviors that lead to improved oral communication. For instance, many SLPs teach people who stutter to control and/or monitor the rate at which they speak. In addition, people may learn to start saying words in a slightly slower and less physically tense manner. They may also learn to control or monitor their breathing. When learning to control speech rate, people often begin by practicing smooth, fluent speech at rates that are much slower than typical speech, using short phrases and sentences. Over time, people learn to produce smooth speech at faster rates, in longer sentences, and in more challenging situations until speech sounds both fluent and natural. "Follow-up" or "maintenance" sessions are often necessary after completion of formal intervention to prevent relapse.

FAST FACT

Stuttering affects about 68 million people worldwide, according to the Stuttering Foundation.

Communicating with People Who Stutter

Often, people are unsure about how to respond when talking to people who stutter. This uncertainty can cause listeners to do things like look away during moments of stuttering, interrupt the person, fill in words, or simply not talk to people who stutter. None of these reactions is particularly helpful, though. In general, people who stutter want to be treated just like anybody else. They are very aware that their speech is different and that it takes them longer to say things. Unfortunately, though, this sometimes leads the person to feel pressure to speak quickly. Under such conditions, people who stutter often have even more difficulty saying what they want to say in a smooth, timely manner. Therefore, listeners who appear impatient or annoyed may actually make it harder for people who stutter to speak.

When talking with people who stutter, the best thing to do is give them the time they need to say what they want to say. Try not to finish sentences or fill in words for them. Doing so only increases the person's sense of time pressure. Also, suggestions like "slow down," "relax," or "take a deep breath" can make the person feel even more uncomfortable because these comments suggest that stuttering should be simple to overcome, but it's not!

Of course, different people who stutter will have different ways of handling their speaking difficulties. Some will be comfortable talking about it with you, while others will not. In general, however, it can be quite helpful to simply ask the person what would be the most helpful way to respond to his or her stuttering. You might say something like, "I noticed that you stutter. Can you tell me how you prefer for people to respond when you stutter?" Often, people will appreciate your interest. You certainly don't want to talk down to them or treat them differently just because they stutter. However, you can still try to find a matter-of-fact, supportive way to let them know that you are interested in *what* they are saying, rather than *how* they're saying it. This can go a long way toward reducing awkwardness, uncertainty, or tension in the situation and make it easier for both parties to communicate effectively.

Aphasia Disrupts Speech and Language Comprehension

National Institute on Deafness and Other Communication Disorders

Aphasia is a speech disorder that disrupts the expression and understanding of language, explains the National Institute on Deafness and Other Communication Disorders (NIDCD). Although children can acquire aphasia, it most often affects older people who have had a stroke or an injury resulting in damage to the speech and language centers of the brain. People with aphasia may have difficulty understanding language and may speak in long sentences that make no sense, or they may comprehend the speech of others but use only very short phrases themselves, states the NIDCD. Speech therapy for aphasia focuses on helping an individual restore language skills or on developing other methods of communication. Computer-assisted therapies as well as experimental drugs show promise in helping people with aphasia recover their language functions.

The NIDCD is a branch of the National Institutes of Health, a division of the US Department of Health and Human Services.

Aphasia is a disorder that results from damage to portions of the brain that are responsible for language. For most people, these are areas on the left side (hemisphere) of the brain. Aphasia usually occurs suddenly, often as the result of a stroke or head injury, but it may also develop slowly, as in the case of a brain tumor, an infection, or dementia. The disorder impairs the expression and understanding of language as well as reading and writing. Aphasia may co-occur with speech disorders such as dysarthria or apraxia of speech, which also result from brain damage.

Anyone can acquire aphasia, including children, but most people who have aphasia are middle-aged or older. Men and women are equally affected. According to the National Aphasia Association, approximately 80,000 individuals acquire aphasia each year from strokes. About one million people in the United States currently have aphasia.

What Causes Aphasia?

Aphasia is caused by damage to one or more of the language areas of the brain. Many times, the cause of the brain injury is a stroke. A stroke occurs when blood is unable to reach a part of the brain. Brain cells die when they do not receive their normal supply of blood, which carries oxygen and important nutrients. Other causes of brain injury are severe blows to the head, brain tumors, brain infections, and other conditions that affect the brain.

There are two broad categories of aphasia: fluent and non-fluent.

Fluent Aphasia

Damage to the temporal lobe (the side portion) of the brain may result in a fluent aphasia called Wernicke's aphasia. In most people, the damage occurs in the left temporal lobe, although it can result from damage to the right lobe as well. People with Wernicke's aphasia may speak in long sentences that have no meaning, add unnecessary words, and even create made-up words. For example, someone with Wernicke's aphasia may say, "You know that smoodle pinkered and that I want to get him round and take care of him like you want before." As a result, it is often difficult to follow what the person is trying to say. People with Wernicke's aphasia usually have great difficulty understanding speech, and they are often unaware of their mistakes. These individuals usually have no body weakness because their brain injury is not near the parts of the brain that control movement.

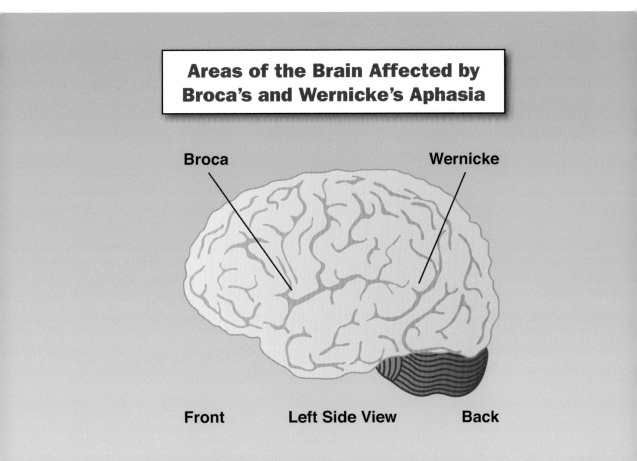

Areas of the Brain Affected by Broca's and Wernicke's Aphasia

Broca

Wernicke

Front   Left Side View   Back

Taken from: National Institute on Deafness and Other Communication Disorders, October 2008.

Non-Fluent Aphasias

A type of non-fluent aphasia is Broca's aphasia. People with Broca's aphasia have damage to the frontal lobe of the brain. They frequently speak in short phrases that make sense but are produced with great effort. They often omit small words such as "is," "and," and "the." For example, a person with Broca's aphasia may say, "Walk dog," meaning, "I will take the dog for a walk," or "book book two table," for "There are two books on the table." People with Broca's aphasia typically understand the speech of others fairly well. Because of this, they are often aware of their difficulties and can become easily frustrated. People with Broca's aphasia often have right-sided weakness or paralysis of the arm and leg because the frontal lobe is also important for motor movements.

Another type of non-fluent aphasia, global aphasia, results from damage to extensive portions of the language areas of the brain. Individuals with global aphasia have severe communication difficulties and may be extremely limited in their ability to speak or comprehend language.

There are other types of aphasia, each of which results from damage to different language areas in the brain. Some people may have difficulty repeating words and sentences even though they can speak and they understand the meaning of the word or sentence. Others may have difficulty naming objects even though they know what the object is and what it may be used for.

FAST FACT

Aphasia affects 1 out of every 250 people. It is more common than cerebral palsy, muscular dystrophy, or Parkinson's disease.

Diagnosing Aphasia

Aphasia is usually first recognized by the physician who treats the person for his or her brain injury. Frequently this is a neurologist. The physician typically performs tests that require the person to follow commands, answer questions, name objects, and carry on a conversation. If the physician suspects aphasia, the patient is often referred to a speech-language pathologist, who performs a comprehensive examination of the person's communication abilities. The examination includes the person's ability to speak, express ideas, converse socially, understand language, read, and write, as well as the ability to swallow and to use alternative and augmentative communication.

Therapy for Aphasia

In some cases, a person will completely recover from aphasia without treatment. This type of spontaneous recovery usually occurs following a type of stroke in which blood flow to the brain is temporarily interrupted but quickly restored, called a transient ischemic attack. In these circumstances, language abilities may return in a few hours or a few days.

For most cases, however, language recovery is not as quick or as complete. While many people with aphasia experience partial spontaneous recovery, in which some language abilities return a few days to a month after the brain injury, some amount of aphasia typically remains. In these instances, speech-language therapy is often helpful. Recovery usually continues over a two-year period. Many health professionals believe that the most effective treatment begins early in the recovery process. Some of the factors that influence the amount of improvement include the cause of the brain damage, the area of the brain that was damaged, the extent of the brain injury, and the age and health of the individual. Additional factors include motivation, handedness, and educational level.

Aphasia therapy aims to improve a person's ability to communicate by helping him or her to use remaining language abilities, restore language abilities as much as possible, compensate for language problems, and learn other methods of communicating. Individual therapy focuses on the specific needs of the person, while group therapy offers the opportunity to use new communication skills in a small-group setting. Stroke clubs, regional support groups formed by people who have had a stroke, are available in most major cities. These clubs also offer the opportunity for people with aphasia to try new communication skills. In addition, stroke clubs can help a person and his or her family adjust to the life changes that accompany stroke and aphasia.

Family involvement is often a crucial component of aphasia treatment so that family members can learn the best way to communicate with their loved one.

Family members are encouraged to:

- Simplify language by using short, uncomplicated sentences.
- Repeat the content words or write down key words to clarify meaning as needed.
- Maintain a natural conversational manner appropriate for an adult.
- Minimize distractions, such as a loud radio or TV, whenever possible.
- Include the person with aphasia in conversations.
- Ask for and value the opinion of the person with aphasia, especially regarding family matters.
- Encourage any type of communication, whether it is speech, gesture, pointing, or drawing.
- Avoid correcting the person's speech.
- Allow the person plenty of time to talk.
- Help the person become involved outside the home; seek out support groups such as stroke clubs.

Other treatment approaches involve the use of computers to improve the language abilities of people with aphasia. Studies have shown that computer-assisted therapy can help people with aphasia retrieve certain parts of speech, such as the use of verbs. Computers can also provide an alternative system of communication for people with difficulty expressing language. Lastly, com-

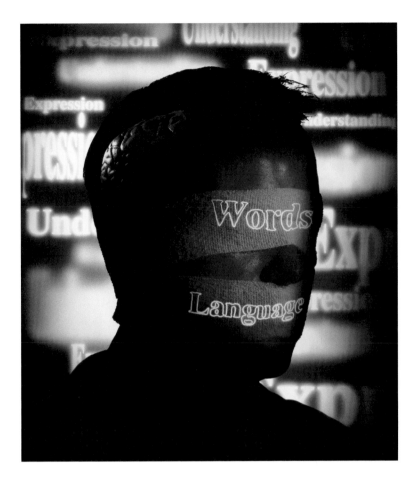

Aphasia is a language impairment affecting the production or comprehension of speech and the ability to read and write. (© **Tim Vernon/ LTH NHS Trust/Photo Researchers, inc.**)

puters can help people who have problems perceiving the difference between phonemes (the sounds from which words are formed) by providing auditory discrimination exercises.

Scientific Explorations

Scientists are attempting to reveal the underlying problems that cause certain symptoms of aphasia. The goal is to understand how injury to a particular part of the brain impairs a person's ability to convey and understand language. The results could be useful in treating various types of aphasia, since the treatment may change depending upon the cause of the language problem.

Other research is attempting to understand the parts of the language process that contribute to sentence comprehension and production and how these parts may break down in aphasia. In this way, it may be possible to pinpoint where the breakdown occurs and help in the development of more focused treatment programs.

Although different languages have many things in common when specific portions of the brain are injured, there are also differences. Scientists are trying to understand the common (or universal) symptoms of aphasia and the language-specific symptoms of the disorder. Other researchers are examining whether people with aphasia may still know their language but have difficulty accessing that knowledge. These studies may help with the development of tests and rehabilitation strategies that focus on specific characteristics of one language or multiple languages.

Researchers are exploring drug therapy as an experimental approach to treating aphasia. Some studies are testing how drugs can be used in combination with speech therapy to improve recovery of various language functions.

Researchers are also looking at how treatment of other cognitive deficits involving attention and memory can improve communication abilities.

To understand recovery processes in the brain, some researchers are using functional magnetic resonance imaging (fMRI) to better understand the human brain regions involved in speaking and understanding language. This type of research may improve understanding of how these areas reorganize after brain injury. The results could have implications for both the basic understanding of brain function and the diagnosis and treatment of neurological diseases.

Selective Mutism Is Both an Anxiety and a Speech Disorder

Neil Izenberg and Steven A. Dowshen

In the following viewpoint medical editors Neil Izenberg and Steven A. Dowshen present an overview of selective mutism, an anxiety disorder that affects a child's speech. Children with selective mutism feel so self-conscious and fearful that they are completely unable to speak in certain situations even though they are able to talk when they feel comfortable. If left untreated, selective mutism may last for years and lead to social anxiety disorder in adulthood, the authors note. Behavioral therapy, which helps people gradually change certain unwanted behaviors, is the most common treatment for this disorder, the authors assert.

Neil Izenberg, a pediatrician, and Dowshen, a pediatric endocrinologist, are both on staff at the Alfred L. Dupont Hospital for Children in Wilmington, Delaware.

When Brandon first started kindergarten, his teacher just thought he was a very quiet boy, that he would come out of his shell in a week or two. As the weeks passed into months, though, Brandon still never spoke a word at school, even when the teacher called on him. Sometimes if he needed something, he would point or gesture, but he would never speak. His teacher was concerned, and when she called his parents, they told her that Brandon spoke easily at home, and that he had always been a little shy around others. It was clear that Brandon's problem was more than normal shyness. Since it was interfering with his ability to participate in class and on the playground, Brandon's parents took him to a mental health professional, who diagnosed his problem as selective mutism.

Selective mutism is a condition in which children feel anxious and inhibited and do not speak in certain situations. Children with selective mutism are capable of speaking normally, and do so in other situations where they feel more comfortable. These children often talk normally at home, but they may completely stop talking around teachers, other children, or other adults. Their behavior gets in the way of making friends and doing well in school.

Selective mutism, once thought to be quite rare, is beginning to be more widely recognized. It used to be called elective mutism, because it was thought that children were purposely choosing not to talk. It was sometimes thought that a child's refusal to speak was a way to rebel against adults, or a sign of anger. It affects at least 1 in 100 school-age children. It usually begins before age 5, but it may not cause problems until children start school. The condition may last for just a few months, but in some cases, if left untreated, selective mutism can last for years. Some experts believe that untreated selective mutism in children leads to social anxiety disorder in their adult years. Experts now believe that selective mutism is an extreme form of social anxiety in a child. Social anxiety is an intense, lasting fear or extreme discomfort in social situations, and usually leads to avoidance of many social situations. With selective mutism, children seem to feel so self-consious or anxious in certain situations that they avoid talking altogether.

Causes and Symptoms

There is no single cause of selective mutism. As with other forms of anxiety, some children may be more likely to have this problem if anxiety or extreme shyness runs in the family, or if they are born with a shy nature. Beyond genetics, in some families where adults are anxious,

Children afflicted with selective mutism feel self-conscious and fearful of speaking in certain situations even though they are relaxed. If untreated it can lead to social anxiety disorder.
(© Oscar Burriel/Photo Researchers, Inc.)

"SELECTIVE-MUTISM," by kittydemonchild, www.deviantart.com. © Nisa Martinez. Reproduced by permission.

children may learn to feel socially anxious by watching the way adults react and behave. Upsetting or stressful events such as divorce, the death of a loved one, or frequent moves may trigger selective mutism in a child who is prone to anxiety.

Many children are shy for a while when they first start kindergarten, but most eventually become comfortable in school, make friends, and talk to the teacher. For those with selective mutism, silence continues and lasts for a month or longer. Some children with selective mutism make gestures, nod, or write notes to communicate. Others use one-syllable words or whispers. Many children with selective mutism are very shy and fearful and may have nervous habits, such as biting their nails. They may cling to their parents and sulk around strangers but might throw temper tantrums and be stubborn and demanding at home. When pushed to speak, they may become stubborn in their refusal. It is sometimes hard for adults to understand that fear, not stubbornness, is at the root of selective mutism, and that children with this condition experience speaking as risky, scary, or dangerous. Understood in this way, it is possible to see a child's stubborn refusal to speak when forced as a strong, but misguided, attempt at self-protection.

Diagnosis and Treatment

Some children with selective mutism will speak to a mental health professional, but others will not. Even if children are silent, though, a skilled professional therapist still can learn a lot by watching how they behave. The therapist also can talk to parents and teachers to find out more about the problem and possible factors that contribute to it. In addition, a number of tests may be needed to exclude other possible causes for failing to speak. These include special medical tests to rule out brain damage, intelligence and academic tests to rule out learning problems, speech and language tests to rule out communication disorders, and hearing tests to rule out hearing loss.

Most children who have selective mutism want to feel comfortable talking. Though they resist efforts to help them talk at first, therapy can be very helpful in treating this problem. The most common treatment for selective mutism is behavioral therapy, which helps people gradually change specific, unwanted types of behavior. For example, after the therapist helps the child to feel comfortable, the child might be rewarded for speaking softly and clearly into a tape recorder. Once they have succeeded at this several times, they can move on to being rewarded for speaking to one child at school. Children who are selectively mute may speak to specific children. They then might be invited to

> **FAST FACT**
>
> Some children with selective mutism also have an expressive language disorder, characterized by a limited vocabulary and grasp of grammar.

participate in a group with the children the selectively mute child speaks to.

Often family therapy is added, which helps identify and change behavior patterns within the family that may play a role in maintaining mutism. When a child has selective mutism, it is common for the family members to speak for the child. While they begin to do this out of love and concern and the desire to be helpful, these patterns must be discontinued to help motivate a reluctant child to begin to speak for herself. Play therapy and drawing are often used to help these children to express their feelings and worries. In addition, some children with selective mutism are prescribed medications used for treating anxiety. These medications help lessen the anxiety that plays an important role in the selectively mute child's behavior, allowing the child to take the risks involved in talking out loud.

CHAPTER 2

Issues and Controversies Surrounding Speech Disorders

Therapy Can Help People Who Stutter Become More Fluent in Their Speech

American Speech-Language-Hearing Association

In the following report, the American Speech-Language-Hearing Association (ASHA) describes some therapies that benefit people who stutter. Speech-language pathologists do not really focus on eliminating stuttering altogether, but rather on minimizing its impact on communication. Thus, stutterers learn behavioral strategies that help them cope with breaks in the flow of their speech, reports ASHA. With time and practice, their speech eventually becomes more fluent. Assistive auditory feedback devices are useful for some people, while others find that support groups help them overcome the burden of stuttering.

ASHA is a professional alliance of audiologists, speech-language pathologists, and speech, language, and hearing scientists.

Photo on previous page. A therapist shapes a girl's mouth to help her make the correct sound. (© Lea Paterson/ Photo Researchers, Inc.)

SOURCE: "Stuttering: Benefits of Speech-Language Pathology Services," ASHA.org. Reprinted with permission from Stuttering: Benefits of Speech-Language Pathology Services. Available from the website of the American Speech-Language-Hearing Association: www.asha.org/public/speech/disorders/stutteringSLPbenefits.htm. All rights reserved.

SLPs [speech-language pathologists] work to help people who stutter lessen the impact or severity of disfluency when it occurs. The goal is not so much to eliminate disruptions in fluency—which many people find difficult to do—but to minimize their impact upon communication when they do occur. People may be taught to identify how they react to or cope with breaks in speech fluency. They learn other reactions that will lead to fluent speech and effective communication. For instance, a person who often produces long, physically tense disfluencies would learn to modify these disfluencies so that they become fleeting, relatively effortless breaks in speech. As people become better at managing fluency in therapy, they practice the newly learned skills in real-life situations.

People usually find that these behavioral strategies are relatively easy to implement during therapy activities. In contrast, people may find that day-to-day fluency management—at least in the early stages of treatment—is hard work! Use of the various fluency management techniques requires mental effort. It is one thing to manage or monitor speech rate in a quiet, controlled setting like a therapy room, but quite another in a noisy, fast-paced office or classroom. For this reason, SLPs often work with family members, teachers, and others on what to expect from therapy. Generally, it is not reasonable to expect that a person who stutters will be able to monitor or control his speech fluency at all times of the day in all situations.

Treatment for Children

Traditionally, there has been some reluctance to treat stuttering during the preschool years. This reluctance has stemmed from at least two sources: the observation that many children "outgrow" stuttering, and the belief that therapy heightens a child's awareness of fluency difficulty which in turn increases the child's risk for persistent stuttering. Current thinking is somewhat different from these traditional views, however. It is now generally agreed that early intervention for stuttering is desirable. That said, an SLP still may recommend a "wait and see" approach for children who have been stuttering for only a few months and who otherwise appear to be unconcerned and at low risk for persistent stuttering. If treatment is recommended for preschoolers, the approaches taken usually are somewhat different from those used with older children and adults. For example, parents may be trained to provide youngsters with feedback about their speech fluency, praising the fluent speech ("That was very smooth!"), and occasionally highlighting instances of disfluent speech ("That sounded a little bumpy"). Parents and/or SLPs may model smooth speech. SLPs teach parents when, where, and how to implement these treatments. Recent research suggests that intervention programs like these are quite effective at reducing, if not eliminating, the symptoms of stuttering with preschoolers.

FAST FACT

Seventy-five percent of children who stutter outgrow the disorder by the time they reach adulthood.

Assistive Devices

In addition to the approaches described above, a variety of assistive devices have been developed to help those who stutter speak more smoothly. Most of these assistive devices alter the way in which an individual hears his or her voice while speaking. The devices often are small, so that they fit in or behind a speaker's ear. Laboratory research suggests that some individuals who stutter speak more fluently when they hear their voice played back to them at a slight delay or at a higher or lower pitch, or when "white noise" is played into their ear as they speak. How effective these devices are in real-life settings continues to be studied. Early findings suggest that some people find some auditory feedback devices very helpful, while others do not. Research is ongoing to identify:

- why some people benefit from the devices more than others
- whether the devices can be made to be more effective
- how much improvement one might expect in fluency when a device is used either alone or with speech therapy
- whether the benefits last over time. . . .

Support Groups

In addition to treatment provided by SLPs, some people who stutter have found help dealing with their stuttering through stuttering self-help and support groups. In general, stuttering support groups are not therapy groups. Instead, they are groups of individuals who are facing similar problems. These individuals work together to help themselves cope with the everyday difficulties of stuttering.

A variety of auditory feedback devices have been developed to help stutterers speak more fluently. Most of these devices alter the way an individual hears his or her voice while speaking. (© **AP Images/ South Bend Tribune, Greg Swiercz**)

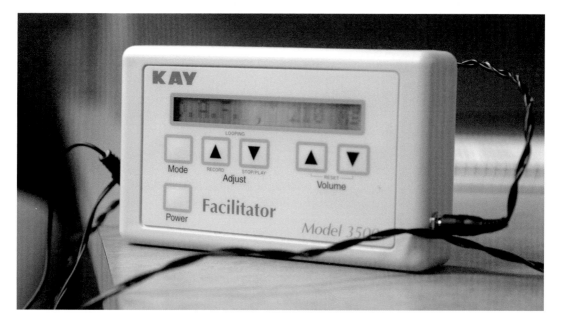

Many such groups exist around the world. In the United States stuttering support groups have a long-standing and strong tradition of helping people overcome the burden of stuttering. Support groups often have local chapters that consist of anywhere from a few to a few dozen members who meet regularly (e.g., weekly or monthly) to discuss issues related to their stuttering. Some groups also have e-mail lists and chat rooms, newsletters and books, and annual conferences that bring together hundreds of people who stutter and their families.

Many support group members report that their experiences in the support group improve their ability to use techniques learned in therapy. Others report that

Developmental Levels of Disfluency

Level of Disfluency	Core Behaviors
Normal Disfluency	Disfluency less than 10 percent of the time, one to two repetitions per instance. Slow, even behaviors.
Borderline Stuttering	Frequency of disfluency increases to more than 10 percent. Repetitions increase to more than two per instance. Repetitions remain loose and relaxed.
Beginning Stuttering	Tense abrupt multiple part-word repetitions. Tense prolongations.
Intermediate Stuttering	Blocks. Repetitions and prolongations continue.
Advanced Stuttering	Blocks. Stoppage of air flow. Tremors from increased duration of blocks.

Taken from: www.coloradostutteringtherapy.com.

the support group meets needs that their formal speech therapy did not meet. Thus, many people benefit from participating in treatment provided by an SLP and a stuttering support group. Indeed, most support groups have developed strong partnerships with the speech-language pathology community to promote and expand treatment options for people who stutter.

Therapy for People Who Stutter Should Focus on Brain Functions Rather than Speech

Barbara Dahm

For the most part, treatment for people who stutter aims toward acceptance or modification of their stuttering. Thus, speech-language pathologists tend to emphasize coping strategies and behavior modification. In the following viewpoint Barbara Dahm presents a new approach to stuttering therapy that focuses on brain functions and the process of producing speech rather than on modifying the symptoms of stuttering. Dahm maintains that dynamic stuttering therapy—a combination of neurological, cognitive, and behavioral strategies—can change how the brain creates speech. With dynamic stuttering therapy, an individual actually learns the processes normally used by speakers to produce speech rather than attempting to accept or control his or her stuttering.

A speech pathologist for over forty years, Dahm is the director of the Communication Therapy Institute in the United States and Israel.

SOURCE: Barbara Dahm, "A New Concept of Stuttering," Stuttering OnlineTherapy.com, June 9, 2010. Copyright © 2010 by Stuttering Online Therapy. All rights reserved. Reproduced by permission.

For the past 60–70 years treatments for stuttering have been based on the concept that stuttering is an uncontrollable thing that happens to people. This "thing" is often described as repetitions, prolongations and blocks that stop the forward flow of speech. Not knowing why and how this happens, the focus has been on the stuttered speech and the consensus for treatment is to accept, control, tame or get rid of it by trying to identify and change the external conditions that are assumed to disrupt speech.

Some conditions that tend to disrupt speech:

- Rate or rhythm of speech
- Fear of stuttering, speaking, or words
- Shame
- Pressure to speak
- Anxiety
- Physical and mental tension
- Lack of control
- Faulty breathing

Over the years this concept of stuttering has become deeply ingrained in the psyche of most people who do and do not stutter. Today it is the basis for most treatments, coping strategies, and advice for people who stutter. In fact it has become so ingrained that ideas that do not fit into this concept are often rejected or not considered serious enough to be investigated.

A Different Concept of Stuttering

Over the past 20 years, while treating people who stutter, a different concept became apparent to me. I realized that there was more to stuttering than meets the eye or ear. The "how" stuttering is created started to emerge. I'd like to share this concept with you.

Within each speaker there is a speech production system and, as in all systems, the way it functions determines the outcome. I came to see stuttering as a breakdown in the way the speech system functions. The result of this breakdown is the variety of symptoms that people who stutter may exhibit.

Symptoms of a breakdown in the speech production system:

- Repetitions, prolongations and blocks in speech
- Facial tension
- Eye blinks
- Loss of eye contact
- Body tension
- Emotional tension
- Low self-esteem
- Uncontrollable movements of body and speech muscles
- Poor vocal quality
- Unclear speech
- Unusual pausing
- And many others

Fortunately, many people have helped me understand stuttering. First and foremost, I have learned so much from listening to and closely observing my clients, and other people who stutter, stuttered and never stuttered. I have also learned a lot from studies on the brain functions of people who stutter, neuroplasticity [the ability of the brain to adapt], and from researchers such as [W.J.M.] Levelt (1989) who describes how normally fluent speech is developed, as well as [A.] Smith & [E.] Kelly (1996); [B.C.] Watson et. al. (1997), who through their research have also come to look at stuttering from the perspective of system function.

A Speech-Processing Approach

It is difficult to change ingrained concepts, because it is human nature to stick with the way we see things. I believe this is the reason that therapy for stuttering has not changed much in 60 years. The focus of therapy then and now is on

stuttering as speech, rather than on the process of producing speech. Over and over again we hear that there are two basic treatment approaches—stuttering modification and fluency shaping. You either learn to live with stuttering or learn how to control or modify stuttering/fluency/speech.

There is an alternative stuttering therapy that doesn't try to solve the problem by treating the symptoms. It focuses on how all of the processes of speech production interact, as well as on all the factors that influence the way the brain functions. I call this a speech-processing approach. In this approach the focus is on changing brain functions so that speaking is virtually effortless and automatic. The treatment guides people who stutter to use their system according to Levelt's model of a normal speech production. Stuttering disappears when the processes function naturally.

Dynamic stuttering therapy involves exploration and self-discovery, identifying changes that must be made and learning how to make them. (© Olivier Voisin/Photo Researchers, Inc.)

The process of normal speaking:

- Attending to the nonverbal idea that the person is expressing
- The brain automatically transforming ideas into language
- The brain simultaneously sending a signal to the speech motor system so that a natural voice that contains intonation is produced
- The mouth simultaneously moving subconsciously and automatically

In normal speech production there is no conscious word awareness, no control over motor activity, and no such thing as trying to "get words out". People who stutter may produce speech in this way some of the time, but it is not their exclusive way of speaking. If it were their speech would not be stuttered.

Dynamic Stuttering Therapy

Changing how the brain creates speech is the goal of the treatment program Dynamic Stuttering Therapy. The treatment process involves exploration and self-discovery, identifying what changes need to be made and learning how to make them. It involves making a commitment to effect neurological, cognitive, and behavioral change, and reinforcing these changes until they become habitual.

The specific goals of therapy that relate to neurological functions are not techniques for controlling speech. They are simply processes normally used by speakers to produce speech.

Specific goals of Dynamic Stuttering Therapy:

1. Learning to develop internal (subvocal speech) naturally without any attempt to get it out
2. Allowing the speech muscles to work on an automatic mode
3. Generating your voice naturally in a way that allows for the expression of mood and meaning

Many people who have learned to use techniques for controlling their stuttering balk at the idea of not using these controls. They say, "Sure I would like to produce speech more automatically, but I need a way to get out of blocks and to control my stutter". It is hard to grasp that the point of learning to produce speech naturally is that when you do it, stuttering doesn't happen. Most people are so locked into their way of thinking that they cannot fathom speaking without effort and thought. They do not realize that there can be a scenario where there is no need for speech controls. Training yourself to function in a new way requires awareness and repetitive use of the brain function. It is moving away from thought about how to say words and control speech toward the automatic expression of thought.

FAST FACT

Famous stutterers include physicist Isaac Newton, author Lewis Carroll, English prime minister Winston Churchill, and actors Marilyn Monroe, Bruce Willis, and James Earl Jones.

Speaking naturally is different; it is possible; it is not physically hard to do and requires no special skills, but changing long held concepts and being open to a new approach is a great human challenge.

People Who Stutter Face Discrimination

William D. Parry

People who stutter frequently experience discrimination in education and employment, writes William D. Parry in the following viewpoint. Stutterers often feel they must hide their disorder on the job; many also encounter negative stereotypes and harassment from supervisors or are denied promotions, the author asserts. Many people have the misguided impression that stutterers are nervous, fearful, indecisive, or mentally unstable—and therefore incapable of dealing with the public or holding leadership positions. Parry maintains that people who stutter should stop attempting to disguise their disorder and let others know that stuttering is not shameful. Moreover, stutterers should insist that employers judge them on their strengths and not stress "communication skills" as an excuse to discriminate against them.

Parry, a speech-language pathologist and trial lawyer, is author of *Understanding and Controlling Stuttering: A Comprehensive New Approach Based on the Valsalva Hypothesis.*

Of the many obstacles faced by people who stutter, perhaps the most devastating is discrimination in employment and educational opportunities. As an NSP [National Stuttering Project] chapter leader and as current chair of the NSP's Advocacy Committee, I have heard from stutterers who try to hide their stuttering on the job for fear of being fired, who suffer harassment or unfavorable evaluations by intolerant supervisors, and who have been denied promotions to supervisory positions or jobs that involve speaking or dealing with the public.

I personally felt the sting of employment discrimination early in my legal career, when I was openly rejected by firms because of my stuttering, despite my academic qualifications. At the recent NSP convention in Atlanta, I heard similar stories, including that of a speech-language pathology student who was told by his Speech Department that he could not graduate unless he stopped stuttering.

I am convinced that discrimination against stutterers is at least as pervasive as racial or sexual discrimination. In some ways it is even more insidious, because: (1) stutterers are a much smaller minority with less political clout; and (2) many people feel justified in assuming that stuttering is a legitimate job disqualification or a sign of incompetence.

Negative Stereotypes

Research has confirmed that persons who stutter are subject to negative stereotypes, which have significantly harmed their employment and promotion opportunities. These stereotypes include the widely accepted impression that stutterers are nervous, shy, quiet, self-conscious, withdrawn, tense, anxious, fearful, reticent, and guarded. For example, one NSP member was denied a promotion by the U.S. Weather Service because his supervisor incorrectly assumed, on the basis of his stuttering, that he lacked the ability "to make rapid fire judgments, think quickly and demonstrate leadership ability."

These negative attitudes have had a significant adverse effect in terms of employment. A 1997 study reported high unemployment for persons who stutter, difficulty in gaining promotions, and a feeling of being discriminated against because of their stuttering. Other studies in 1983 showed that both employers and vocational rehabilitation counselors perceived stuttering to be a vocationally disabling disorder. In a 1991 study, employers reported that, while stuttering does not hinder a person's performance, it does inhibit his or her ability to gain employment or a promotion.

Studies have shown that these negative views of persons who stutter are shared by almost all groups studied—students, teachers, employers, parents, even speech-language pathologists. Even worse, studies show that persons who stutter also believe these stereotypes and tend to behave accordingly. It seems that people who stutter are not only victims of the stereotype, but they themselves may help to perpetuate it. Therefore, we must begin by correcting our own attitudes, if we are to succeed in dispelling the prejudices of others.

Self-Defeating Behaviors

Ironically, the negative image of stutterers may be made even worse by our attempts to avoid or to disguise our stuttering. For example, rather than acknowledging a block, we might pretend that we have forgotten the word, can't decide what to say, or don't know the answer to a question. Or we might engage in inappropriate word substitutions or circumlocutions. While we may think we have fooled people by doing this, we really haven't. We have merely confirmed the stereotype that stutterers are hesitant, indecisive, or stupid.

In terms of listener reaction, research has shown that trying to hide our stuttering is actually the worst thing

"Will that be all, or would you like to add a few more ums, ers and ahs?," cartoon by Elmer Parolini, www.cartoonstockcom. Copyright © Elmer Parolini. Reproduction rights obtainable from www.CartoonStock.com.

we can do. Studies have shown that listeners have a much more favorable impression of stutterers who acknowledge their stuttering than of stutters who do not. Listeners also have a more favorable reaction to actual stuttering blocks, repetitions, and prolongations than to the kind of interjections (um's and ah's, etc.) that we often use when we try to avoid stuttering.

Therefore, if we are to break the negative stereotypes, we must accept and acknowledge our stuttering. We must come "out of the closet" and let employers and others know that stuttering is no stigma and nothing to be ashamed of. For example, we should freely discuss our involvement with the NSP and wear our NSP buttons with pride. If we act as if we are ashamed of ourselves and our stuttering, how can we expect others to treat us with respect?

Educating the Public

Despite two decades of publicity about stuttering's possible neurological and hereditary factors, the popular idea that stuttering is caused by "nervousness" continues to persist. Studies indicate that this is due to people's tendency to equate stuttering with their own moments of disfluency—which may have been prompted by nervousness, fear, uncertainty or emotional conflict. They assume that the stutterer is experiencing similar feelings—only more so. Consequently, they may view stutterers as being nervous, slow, ineffectual, indecisive, or mentally unstable.

We must be ready to disabuse people of these harmful and incorrect assumptions by explaining stuttering in terms that they can understand and relate to. It might be helpful to formulate a brief explanation of stuttering in advance. Ideally, such an explanation should be simple enough to fit into a 15-second sound bite, yet concrete enough for people to conceptualize and remember. Of necessity, it cannot be as complete or sophisticated as speech professionals would like or satisfy all of their competing theories. However, it should offer a credible alternative to displace the shame, stigma, and negative stereotypes associated with stuttering.

Emphasizing Normalcy

While emphasizing that stuttering involves neurological factors, rather than being caused by "nervousness" or emotional problems, we must also be careful not to create the negative impression that stutterers are seriously brain-damaged or otherwise defective. Instead, we should eliminate the shame and stigma of stuttering by emphasizing the stutterer's basic normality.

I personally have had success in explaining stuttering to people by telling them that it is not caused by nervousness, but that it might involve, among other things, "a neurological confusion between two basically normal bodily functions—speech and the Valsalva mechanism." I explain that when I feel that speaking may be difficult, I tend to activate the Valsalva mechanism—which is a bodily mechanism that everybody normally uses to help them to exert effort or to force things out of the body, but which causes a blockage of speech. I might then have them perform a simple exercise which activates the Valsalva mechanism, causing them to personally experience physical blockage in the mouth or larynx—similar to what may happen during a stuttering block. While this explanation mentions only one of many possible factors involved in stuttering, it has the advantage of focusing on a normal bodily function that people can personally experience and remember. It also allows for a discussion of stuttering in terms that are free of any possible shame or stigma.

> **FAST FACT**
>
> Over 3 million people in the United States stutter.

Standing Up for Our Rights

Our right to equal opportunity should not be conditioned upon our fluency. We should have the right to accept our stuttering and to insist that employers judge us solely upon our ability to perform the essential requirements of the job in question.

We should not allow employers to put undue emphasis on "communication skills" as a pretext for discriminating against stuttering. Employers must learn that (except perhaps in the most severe cases) stuttering need not interfere with effective communication! The greatest obstacle to communication comes when we feel compelled to hide our stuttering out of fear of reprisal. For employers to demand fluency as the price of one's job only creates a vicious spiral of stress and anxiety that makes stuttering worse.

When all else fails, we must be ready to use legal remedies to challenge acts of discrimination. A number or state and federal statutes now outlaw discrimination against persons with handicaps or disabilities, which may offer protections to persons who stutter. Most recently, the Americans with Disabilities Act of 1990 ("ADA") banned discrimination "against qualified individuals because of a disability, in regard to job application procedures, hiring, advancement, discharge, compensation, job training, and other terms, conditions, and privileges of employment." Each statute has its own specific terms, applicability, and procedures, which must be followed precisely.

Legal Cases Must Be Carefully Planned

Unfortunately, discrimination cases are usually very hard to win, even for experienced attorneys, so they should not be undertaken haphazardly. Although a number of stut-

The 1990 Americans with Disabilities Act was signed by President George H.W. Bush. Although the act banned discrimination against qualified individuals because of a disability, stutterers may still face discrimination. (© Fotosearch/Getty Images)

tering discrimination cases have been successfully settled before trial, the question of whether stuttering is legally a "disability" entitled to protection is still undecided by the courts. Our greatest fear is that poorly prepared cases will result in unfavorable judicial opinions, which will then be followed by courts in other cases and seriously damage the rights of all persons who stutter.

Therefore, it is important that the NSP's Advocacy Committee be notified of all stuttering discrimination cases, as soon as they are brought or contemplated, so that we can provide whatever advice and assistance might be appropriate.

Because stuttering is such a complex and misunderstood disorder, stuttering discrimination cases must be carefully planned and prepared in order to avoid potential disaster. It would be a tragedy if we allowed the popular prejudices and misconceptions about stuttering to become enshrined as judicial precedent, leaving millions of persons who stutter without legal protection.

Many People Who Stutter Have Successful Careers

The Stuttering Foundation

The following selection is excerpted from a brochure addressing employers and human-resource professionals. In it, the Stuttering Foundation points out that people who stutter are successful in a wide variety of occupations, including careers that require leadership skills and daily contact with the public. People who stutter are often very adept at verbal communication and have the same ambitions as nonstutterers; thus they should be offered the same opportunities that would be offered to anyone else who is qualified for a position, asserts the author. In addition, people who stutter should honestly inform their employers about how their disorder might affect some aspects of their job performance as well as how their strengths would be of benefit, the Stuttering Foundation claims. Stutterers are encouraged to undergo professional therapy and self-guided therapy. The Stuttering Foundation is a nonprofit organization that provides services and support to people who stutter and their families.

SOURCE: "Stuttering: Answers for Employers," StutteringHelp.org, July 2007. Copyright © 2007 by The Stuttering Foundation. All rights reserved. Reproduced by permission.

The Stuttering Foundation receives many requests each year from managers, human resources professionals, and business owners for more information about stuttering. We assembled this guide to answer some common questions about stuttering and to provide additional resources for people who stutter and their colleagues in the workplace.

Basic Facts

- Over three million Americans stutter—more than one adult in a hundred. Stuttering affects 3 to 4 times as many men as women.
- There is a very good chance that your organization employs or will employ people who stutter.
- Stuttering is a chronic communication disorder that interferes with a person's ability to speak fluently. While the cause of stuttering is not known, there is evidence that the disorder has strong genetic and neurological components.
- People who stutter have performed successfully in the widest range of occupations—from teacher to medical doctor and from public relations executive to salesperson.
- Many men and women who stutter have gone on to have highly successful careers in their chosen fields.

FAST FACT

Stuttering is found in every culture and language. The primary language of the speaker does not increase or decrease the amount of stuttering.

Eliminating Stereotypes About Stuttering

- People who stutter are as intelligent and well-adjusted as those who don't.
- Don't assume that people who stutter are prone to be nervous, anxious, fearful, or shy. While stuttering behaviors may sometimes resemble the behaviors of those who experience these emotions, people who stutter exhibit the same full range of personality traits as those who do not.
- Stuttering is not the result of emotional conflict or fearfulness.

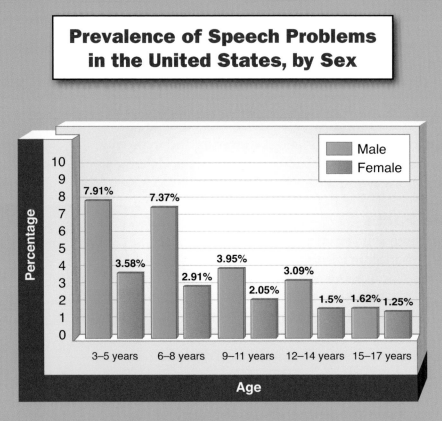

Prevalence of Speech Problems in the United States, by Sex

Male
Female

Percentage

7.91% 3.58% 7.37% 2.91% 3.95% 2.05% 3.09% 1.5% 1.62% 1.25%

3–5 years   6–8 years   9–11 years   12–14 years   15–17 years

Age

Taken from: National Institute on Deafness and Other Communication Disorders, based on data from the National Survey of Children's Health, 2003.

- People who stutter often have excellent communications skills. They should not be seen as deficient at verbal communication. Some are very often qualified for and interested in positions requiring them to deal with members of the public on a daily basis.
- People who stutter have the same ambitions and goals for advancement as non-stutterers. To an extent consistent with their abilities, they should be offered leadership opportunities and paths for promotion within an organization.
- Stuttering varies widely in different people and varies in the same person over different times and places. People who stutter often have "good" and "bad" days with their speech.

- For people who stutter, a job interview is perhaps the single most difficult speaking situation they will ever encounter and is not indicative of how they would speak on the job. It is important to consider the actual job requirements and conditions.
- Some people who stutter less severely may not acknowledge it publicly for fear of losing their jobs or being denied promotions. By feeling forced to keep their condition a secret, they place themselves under enormous stress. This can impact their own job performance as well as that of their colleagues.

Helpful Strategies

- Employee Assistance Programs (EAPs) can be very helpful by maintaining information on stuttering so that employees with questions—for themselves and their children—can be referred to the appropriate professionals.

For stutterers, a job interview is the single most difficult speaking situation they encounter. However, it is not indicative of how they will speak on the job. (© **Corbis Flirt/Alamy**)

• The best way to approach an employee's stuttering is through honest communication. By refraining from making assumptions about the person's job-related abilities and skills, both the employee and employer can effectively achieve their goals.

Responsibilities of People Who Stutter

• The Stuttering Foundation encourages people who stutter to take an active approach towards their stuttering. This includes professional therapy as well as self therapy. The Foundation offers a nationwide referral list of specialists in stuttering and information to help people obtain insurance coverage. It also has effective self therapy materials. . . .

• People who stutter should be honest and open with their employers about their speaking abilities and the areas in which they feel they can perform effectively. They should be willing to discuss how their disability might impact particular areas of their job performance, and what might be done to accommodate their disability.

Repetitive Books Are Useful Tools for Treating Childhood Apraxia of Speech

Michelle Solomon and Lavinia Pereira

In the selection that follows, Michelle Solomon and Lavinia Pereira explain the benefits of predictable, repetitive books as therapy for children diagnosed with apraxia of speech. Such books invite children to participate more in reading by filling in words or phrases, and the recurring words and repeated content provide numerous opportunities to practice certain sounds. In effect, these books help children with apraxia learn to associate sounds with symbols, and success with reading boosts their self-esteem, the authors explain.

Solomon, a speech-language pathologist (SLP) with a private practice in New York, instructs speech therapists on therapy techniques. Pereira, also an SLP with a private practice in New York, holds a position as a clinical supervisor of graduate students at New York University. Both authors are the creators of the First Sound series of interactive children's books that foster the development and growth of speech and language skills.

Books are an excellent tool in treatment for speech and language disorders due to the multi-sensory approach they provide for learning. All books encourage speech and language development; however, which books provide the most beneficial treatment for children diagnosed with Childhood Apraxia of Speech (CAS)? In the treatment of CAS, it is generally understood that frequent practice of sounds and words helps to improve speech and reduce some of the pressures associated with expressive language. Repetitive books contain various characteristics that can be part of an effective treatment strategy for children diagnosed with CAS—predictability, presence of carrier phrases, frequent practice of target sounds, familiar inflection, and an introduction to phonemic awareness.

Young children's favorite books are usually highly predictable. A repetitive book may be predictable in a variety of ways; the story may repeat itself, a portion of a phrase may appear on each page or the same question may be asked throughout. The predictable design of many repetitive books allows the child to grasp the content of the story with greater ease, decreasing the "cognitive load" that may come with reading a narrative type story. When the child has less to think about, often the easier it is to verbally express their thoughts.

Fill-Ins and Recurring Words

In addition, predictable children's books utilize a cloze procedure which allows a child to fill in words, phrases, and character's names, as the book content becomes more familiar. Non-repetitive books often result in the child attempting to participate in reading by either imitating the readers' words or by answering questions presented by the reader. A predictable repetitive book allows the child to fill in without imitating; a skill very difficult for most children with CAS. The ability to fill in words and phrases can lead to increased participation, turn taking, and decreased frustration for the child.

In repetitive books, there will often be a functional carrier phrase used throughout the story. For example, the popular book, "Brown Bear, Brown Bear" contains the carrier phrase "I see a ___ looking at me". These phrases allow the child to produce a longer utterance while only having to change one core word. As a result, an unlimited number of multiword utterances may be created. A child with CAS often presents with decreased intelligibility as the length of an utterance increases. By practicing carrier phrases, the child can develop the motor plan for the portion of the phrase that repeats itself, in turn decreasing the "motor load" required for a lengthier utterance. As with predictability, these phrases allow the child to experience increased participation as well as the success of producing multi-word utterances.

The presence of carrier phrases, repeated content and recurring words in a repetitive book can result in the frequent occurrence of a particular sound (phoneme) or

In the treatment of childhood apraxia of speech, the use of books to practice sounds and words helps improve speech and reduces some of the pressures associated with expressive language. (© Ellen B. Senisi/Photo Researchers, Inc.)

Symptoms That May Indicate Childhood Apraxia

The child:

- does not coo or babble as an infant
- begins speaking late
- only voices a few different consonant and vowel sounds
- struggles combining sounds
- has problems eating
- has difficulty imitating speech
- sounds choppy, monotonous, and difficult to understand
- appears to be groping when attempting to speak

Taken from: Nationwide Children's Hospital. "Childhood Apraxia of Speech Cases on the Rise." *Science Daily*, October 2007.

group of sounds. A child with CAS often presents with difficulty producing even the smallest unit of speech. If a particular phoneme is featured in a repetitive book, the child will be provided with numerous opportunities to practice the motor plan for that phoneme in a functional and interactive approach. As with other speech motor activities such as counting and reciting the alphabet, the more the child practices the motor plan necessary for production, the more automatic it becomes. The increased practice can result in improved production of a sound, syllable or word and increased confidence when attempting to communicate. Error inconsistency, a characteristic often cited for children with CAS, may decrease in the context of a repetitive book due to the frequent practice.

Improving Prosody

Familiar inflection, another characteristic of repetitive books, can assist in addressing some of the difficulties

PERSPECTIVES ON DISEASES AND DISORDERS

with prosody that children with CAS experience. Prosody is defined [by researchers C. Chamberlain and R. Strode] as "the stress, duration, pitch, rate, and timing changes that make our speech meaningful, intelligible, and interesting. It is the melody of speech." These [prosodic] features are often sacrificed resulting in decreased intelligibility, difficulty expressing emotion through speech inflection, effortful speech, robotic sounding speech and equalized stress patterns. As a reader recites a repetitive book it is instinctive to apply an almost sing song like or melodic tone to the books' phrases. Each time a phrase, question or sequence of words is repeated the same inflection, rate, pitch and stress pattern may be applied when read aloud. In turn, as the child begins to fill in words, phrases and recite patterns of the story, they may attempt to apply the same patterns resulting in improved prosody.

> ## FAST FACT
>
> Some children with verbal apraxia lick their hands to indicate that they are hungry or thirsty.

Repetitive books foster the development of phonemic awareness and sound symbol association. Children with Apraxia are often at risk for language and reading delays. Developing sound symbol awareness and early sight word recognition can be challenging and frustrating for the child. A repetitive book, particularly those with repeated words and short phrases can assist in the development of phonemic awareness and pre-reading skills.

The predictability, use of carrier phrases, frequent practice of a target sound(s), and familiar inflection of repetitive books may help to target some of the characteristics often associated with CAS. The use of repetitive books by therapists as well as by caregivers can offer opportunities for increased participation, decreased frustration, and additional motor planning practice for speech sound production. Successful experiences communicating can improve self-esteem and provide a sense of empowerment.

Eclectic Approaches Are Useful for Treating Childhood Apraxia of Speech

Sharon Gretz

There is no single treatment that is right for every child with apraxia of speech, asserts Sharon Gretz in the following selection. Experienced speech-language pathologists generally prefer an eclectic approach that includes multiple methods based on the child's needs, such as therapy with rhythm and melody, sensory cueing, repetition, picture books, and sign language, Gretz says. While childhood apraxia may co-occur with other disorders, including motor and sensory difficulties, most children with apraxia can make improvements in their speech with the help of a conscientious therapist, the author concludes.

Gretz is the founder and executive director of the Childhood Apraxia of Speech Association of North America. She is also the parent of a child diagnosed with apraxia of speech.

Apraxia of speech is considered a motor speech disorder. For unknown reasons, children with apraxia have great difficulty planning and producing the precise, highly refined and specific series of movements of the tongue, lips, jaw and palate that are necessary for intelligible speech. Apraxia of speech may also be called verbal apraxia, developmental apraxia of speech, or verbal dyspraxia. No matter what it is called the most important concept is the root word "praxis." Praxis means planned movement. So to some degree or another, a child with the diagnosis of apraxia of speech has difficulty programming and planning speech movements. Apraxia of speech is a specific speech disorder.

A true developmental delay of speech is when the child is following the "typical" path of childhood speech development, albeit at a rate slower than normal. Sometimes this rate is commensurate with cognitive skills. In typical speech/language development, the child's receptive and expressive skills are pretty much moving together. What is generally seen in a child with apraxia of speech is a significant gap between their receptive language abilities and expressive abilities. In other words, the child's ability to understand language (receptive ability) is broadly within normal limits, but his or her expressive speech is seriously deficient, absent, or severely unclear. This is an important factor and one indicator that the child may be experiencing more than "delayed" speech and should be evaluated for the presence of a specific speech disorder such as apraxia. However, certain language disorders may also cause a similar pattern in a child. A gap between a child's expressive and receptive language ability is insufficient to diagnose apraxia.

> **FAST FACT**
>
> Children with apraxia of speech often have oral-motor weakness and benefit from exercises that strengthen the face, tongue, and mouth.

The Prognosis for Apraxia of Speech

Prognosis means how the child might be expected to do in the future if he or she receives proper treatment. The answer to this question is that outcomes vary, however, children with apraxia of speech can and do improve! The factors that appear to contribute to prognosis include:

- individual characteristics of the child; these include receptive ability, cognitive ability, desire to communicate (communication intent), age at which appropriate treatment is begun (preschool age being desirable), and attention span;
- the extent to which other medical, speech and/or language issues are present;
- the extent to which therapy is tailored to the unique issues present in the child;
- the extent of family participation and involvement in therapy and follow-through at home.

With appropriate help, most children with apraxia of speech make wonderful gains in their expressive speech ability. However, it is also true that in some situations, despite everyone's best attempts, a child may not evolve to be primarily a verbal communicator.

Be careful of those who want to make detailed projections regarding how your child will do in the future, especially if they have not worked with or gotten to know your child.

Effective Treatments

It is possible to speak only generally about effective therapy practices. Unfortunately, research into effective methods for providing treatment to children with apraxia is limited. However, in the professional literature various techniques described, including PROMPT method, Integral Stimulation, Adapted Cueing, Touch Cue, Melodic Intonation Therapy, Rate Control Therapy, etc. Although these therapeutic approaches differ somewhat, they do have common features. Most notably these include:

- principles of motor learning such as a high degree of practice and repetition, correction and feedback, slowed rate, and a focus on targeted motor placement and productions;

- heightened sensory input for control of the movement sequences and sensory cueing such as visual, tactile, and kinesthetic cueing; touch cueing; verbal cueing;
- use of rhythm and melody;
- focus on speech movements versus individual sounds.

Many experienced speech-language pathologists [SLPs] use an eclectic approach rather than a "one approach fits all" notion, incorporating many of the methods mentioned above and using them based on the individual child's needs. There is no one "program" that is right for every child with apraxia and commercial products and programs

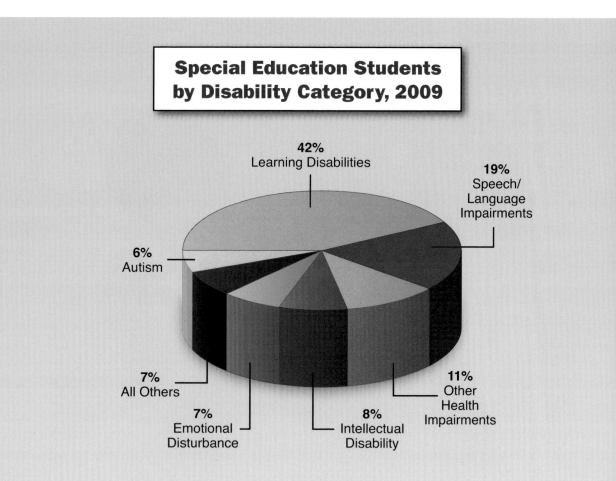

Special Education Students by Disability Category, 2009

42% Learning Disabilities

19% Speech/ Language Impairments

6% Autism

7% All Others

7% Emotional Disturbance

8% Intellectual Disability

11% Other Health Impairments

Taken from: 2009 Child Count, Ages 6–21. www.IDEAdata.org.

can be tools for use in therapy by an SLP who understands the nature of apraxia and how to treat it. However, such programs are not alone the solution.

Children with apraxia of speech reportedly do not progress well in their actual speech production with therapy tailored for other articulation problems or with language stimulation approaches. Additionally, in young children the motor/sensory techniques, drills, etc. should be woven into play activities that are highly motivational to them. What experienced therapists and families report is that children with apraxia need frequent one-on-one therapy and lots of repetition of sounds, sound sequences, and movement patterns in order to incorporate them and make them automatic.

Also, many therapists recommend the use of sign language, picture books, and other means to augment speech in the child who is not clearly understood. This approach

Pathologists treating children in apraxia therapy use motor/sensory techniques and drills woven into play activities that are highly motivational to the children. (© Véronique Burger/Photo Researchers, Inc.)

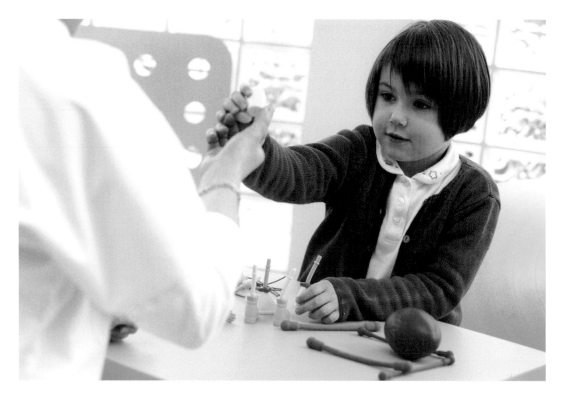

may be called "total communication." Having the child pair a vocal word attempt with a sign enhances the chance that the listener will be able to "catch" the communication (if the spoken word isn't understood, perhaps the sign will be). Having others understand the communication can offer the child motivation and the feeling of success in using their voice to communicate. Many children with apraxia of speech, even at young ages, have some awareness of their difficulty. Providing successful communication experiences only encourages the child. Also, for children with apraxia of speech, signs can become important visual cues to help them know how to place their mouths, etc. in order to produce the desired word. When pairing of spoken word and sign is consistent, the child may come to associate the visual image of the sign with the placement of their articulators. Parents should not be afraid about using sign language with their child. Children will drop the signs on their own as their speech becomes understood. . . .

Will They Speak Normally?

With appropriate therapy and a lot of follow-through by parents and others, many children with apraxia of speech can become effective verbal communicators. Will speech ever be entirely "normal"? We can report that we know of children who ultimately become good speakers and their "problem" is not detectable to nonprofessionals. In other children, lingering articulation issues follow them. Childhood Apraxia of speech is a serious and challenging speech disorder. A lot of hard work on the part of therapist, parents, and child needs to occur. . . .

Co-Occurring Disorders

Some report that "pure" apraxia of speech is quite rare. It appears that frequently children may experience other speech/language issues in addition to the apraxia. For instance, a child may have both apraxia and dysarthria, another motor speech problem involving weakness or paralysis to some degree or another. We know that apraxia of speech may be accompanied by diagnoses such as autism, Down syndrome, or cerebral palsy. Some children with apraxia of speech go on to experience difficulties in reading, spelling, or math while others do not. Many children with apraxia of speech also have fine motor difficulties with their hands, making certain tasks more difficult. Others do not have these problems. Some children experience sensory-related issues as well as apraxia of speech. These children may have sensitivities to sound, clothing, textures, getting their hands messy, etc. They may also have sensory integration difficulties in which they lack awareness of where their bodies are in space or are awkward or uncoordinated. Some recent studies indicate that other developmental concerns are likely in children with a diagnosis of CAS.

The Need for Expertise

It is important to know that not all speech-language pathologists are equally skilled in providing treatment to children with apraxia of speech. Some are better trained than others are and some have evolved their expertise through years of experience. Parents should look for a speech-language pathologist who has experience and success in working with children with apraxia of speech.

Children with Selective Mutism Need Therapy That Addresses Dysfunctional Family Dynamics

Lynda Zielinski

When a child has the capacity for speech but is unable to speak in certain situations, he or she is suffering from selective mutism, writes Lynda Zielinski in the following article. It is thought to be a rare disorder; however, many parents of children with selective mutism do not seek treatment because they think it is a minor problem. Mutism may first be noticed in school settings, as in the case of a sensitive child who stops speaking because of fear of ridicule, Zielinski says. But mutism in the home may be a child's way of expressing anger at feeling wronged or rejected. Professional help is needed, especially in cases of severe and prolonged mutism, asserts the author. Therapists can help to sort out dysfunctional family dynamics—neglect, mistreatment, or other issues—that may be triggering the disorder.

Zielinski is a teacher, social worker, and writer who has been published in *Newsweek* and *Ms.*

As much as it hurts to have a child burst out in an angry tirade, there's another behavior that can be even more painful for a parent—the silent treatment.

When carried to extreme, mental health professionals have a name for it: Selective Mutism. The child with this disorder is capable of speech but doesn't speak. The child is not developmentally delayed, autistic, or hearing impaired. He does not have a physical problem that prevents him from speaking; he just doesn't talk. That's not to say it's a clear conscious choice, it isn't. Like other psychological problems, it has precursors and underlying symptoms. Selective mutism is more than meets the eye—or the ear, in this case.

Definition

Selective Mutism is a childhood disorder characterized as a failure to speak in some situations despite speaking in others. The disorder has to continue for over a month and interfere with normal social interactions to fit the diagnosis. The term "selective" indicates the child talks in some environments but not others, perhaps at home, but not in school, or on the playground, but not in the classroom. The point is that adults know the child can talk; they've heard him, but they don't know why he won't talk.

Selective Mutism is thought to be rare. The syndrome occurs in only 1% of clients who are seen by mental health professionals, according to the Diagnostic and Statistical Manual of Mental Disorders, IV. However, parents may not seek treatment; they may not think it a serious problem.

Mutism at School

The syndrome may start in children as young as five but sometimes is not noticed until the child is in school and his teachers alert the parents.

Not speaking at school can be triggered by a variety of reasons—fear of ridicule is one. A sensitive child may be afraid of saying the wrong thing and getting laughed at. This is more likely to occur in an only child who hasn't had much exposure to other children. An anxious child may feel inhibited and insecure at school. Also, a child with a speech impediment, such as a lisp or a stammer, is more vulnerable to this form of anxiety. If a child does not speak because he is not comfortable with the English language, he usually only needs more time and exposure to the language. However, if in the interim, the child mispronounces words and becomes embarrassed and self-conscious, it may lead to a problem.

> **FAST FACT**
>
> When she was eight years old, American writer Maya Angelou had selective mutism after experiencing sexual abuse. Her speech returned after about a year.

Selective Mutism that occurs at school can be alleviated with cooperation on everyone's part. The teacher needs to instill a helpful attitude on the part of classmates but not go overboard and make the child an oddity. Parents should be patient and reassure the child that he will eventually feel more at ease. If his anxiety is severe, the parent may want to talk to the child's doctor about medication.

It's important to remember that drawing attention to a child's speech is not helpful. Correcting a child or repeating words she mispronounces could make her more self-conscious. The purpose of speech is to communicate. When the child's manner of speaking is more important than the meaning, the child becomes frustrated and speech may become inhibited.

Mutism at Home

Communicating is a need we all have. Children normally want to engage adults, sometimes they chatter to the point of annoyance. But what happens when a child refuses to speak to a parent? This behavior can have ominous consequences. Perhaps the child feels he has been rejected or wronged and uses silence as his weapon. Feeling hurt and angry, he takes his upset out on a parent, most often the mother, although she may not even be the source of his problem. He wants someone to feel his pain.

Nothing is more hurtful than having someone you love refuse to speak to you. The mother naturally responds with hurt and anger. She becomes emotionally 'out of control,' alternately yelling and pleading with the child to get a response. Permitting the child to have so much emotional power over an adult is unhealthy—for everyone. It upsets the rest of the family to witness this emotional tug of war. Everyone becomes exasperated, feeling angry and helpless.

Getting Help

The parent and the child who suffer from this syndrome need professional help to break the cycle. If the mutism is severe and entrenched, as is the case for abused and neglected children, the therapist may need to see the child alone in order to gain his trust. In most cases the parent and child will come in together, or the entire family will be seen. It is not the therapist's job to get the youngster to talk. The therapist will get to know the family. She will find out what's been going on. Sometimes the therapy starts with the parent denying any problems ("We're all fine, he just won't talk.")

In most cases problems gradually emerge. The child has been left home alone, or spends most evenings in the care of a sitter who is less than nurturing. A family member has a substance abuse problem and frightens the child. The child gets blamed for things committed by an older sibling, or gets mistreated by a sibling. The mother has been stressed and has taken it out on the child. She hoped he would forget about it. Once the floodgates have opened, the dynamic of the parent-child relationship changes. The problems can be addressed. The child feels nurtured and protected. The parent can once again connect with the child.

Unfortunately, not all cases of selective mutism receive help. Sometimes in the records of delinquents and teens with mental health problems are written accounts of the child refusing to talk at some earlier time. Parents who are overwhelmed with their own problems, who are stressed by work commitments, and who have other children to worry about, may minimize the problem. Sometimes they look the other way, thinking, "He'll grow out of it, or, one of these days he'll really need me, then he'll snap out of it."

They may be right. The mutism may be a phase. But sometimes different problems follow. At worst, the mutism persists and the child grows into a silent loner. He continues to hold in his anger and upset and doesn't connect with others. He breaks his silence only when he can no longer contain his rage. That's a scary scenario.

It's important to remember that the child is troubled and not bad. Selective mutism may be rare, but we must recognize it and get help for the child early on.

Selective mutism is a childhood disorder characterized by a failure to speak in some situations. It is usually not discovered until the child starts school. (© Corbis Flirt/ Alamy)

Dysfunctional Family Dynamics Do Not Cause Selective Mutism

Christine Stanley

In the following selection, Christine Stanley maintains that there are several myths about selective mutism that need to be debunked. One of them is the notion that selective mutism is very rare; the author contends that it is actually more prevalent than disorders such as autism and cystic fibrosis. In addition, there is no evidence that selective mutism is the result of abuse, neglect, trauma, or dysfunctional family dynamics. Selective mutism most likely has a biological basis rooted in anxiety, Stanley explains, and potential threats may trigger overly anxious reactions, such as mutism, in sensitive individuals. Incorrect ideas about selective mutism are damaging, particularly when parents must risk false accusations of abuse when seeking treatment for their children. There is hope for those living with this disorder as scientific knowledge replaces misinformation, the author concludes.

Stanley is the executive director of the nonprofit Selective Mutism Group, a division of the Childhood Anxiety Network.

Although it was first described 125 years ago (and labeled aphasis voluntaria at that time by a German doctor, [Adolph] Kussmaul), relatively little has been studied or written about the childhood anxiety disorder now known as Selective Mutism [SM]. In reading through the sparse body of literature in textbooks and journals, it is not difficult to see why so many selectively mute children are being misdiagnosed and receiving inadequate or inappropriate therapy.

Unfortunately, many inaccurate theories about the cause and basis of selective mutism have gained acceptance among medical and educational professionals in spite of the lack of supportive evidence. In the vacuum of inadequate research, it seems that these myths have arisen to fill the void of true knowledge and understanding.

Because many of the older theories about selective mutism are currently contributing to the confusion and inappropriate treatment of children with this disorder, this article is an attempt to debunk the following myths.

False Assumptions

Myth #1: Selective mutism is extremely rare.

The most recent study showed a prevalence rate for Selective Mutism of 7.1 per 1,000 children. Older surveys ranged from 0.08%, or 0.8 per 1,000, to 1.8 per 1,000 children. Variation may be due to the methods of surveying used, the age of the children in the sample population, or inadequate recognition of symptoms by parents, medical, and educational professionals. Lack of knowledge about selective mutism leads to many of these children being labeled as "just shy" or misdiagnosed as autistic, so that any reports of the number of cases are likely to be falsely low.

Even the lower estimates show that SM is more common than other childhood disorders such as autism, cystic fibrosis, spina bifada, and muscular dystrophy. Presumably because of greater public awareness, though, these have received much more funding for research and thus are better understood.

Myth #2: Selectively mute children are typically severely emotionally disturbed, usually because they have suffered abuse, neglect or trauma.

This assumption is often seen in older case reports, although no evidence is offered; instead, there is an apparent presumption that children would not exhibit excessive fearfulness in social interactions unless their life experiences had taught them to react in that way. Recent advances in understanding the neurobiological circuitry of anxiety have given reason to believe that human beings are hard-wired to be vigilant to danger, and that in some individuals the gating mechanisms for this circuitry are overly sensitive. Thus, for these individuals, normal life events do trigger anxious responses in certain contexts.

The fear of being placed under suspicion of abuse may prevent parents from seeking help for their children. While there may be a legitimate concern that selectively mute children would be unable to speak out if they were victims of abuse, there is no reason to assume that such abuse is any more likely to be occurring with these children than with the average child.

Not a Family Pathology

Myth #3: Families of children with selective mutism are typically dysfunctional.

While epidemiological studies have shown a high incidence of social anxiety and other forms of anxiety and/or depression in the close relatives of selectively mute individuals, there is no evidence that family pathology causes the symptoms of selective mutism. Discussions in older literature characterize parents, particularly mothers, as being either poorly attached or overly attached to selectively mute children. This notion is very similar to the now-discarded theory about autism that was prevalent several decades ago, when poor maternal bonding was thought to be the cause of that disorder. In both cases, it is likely that any observed bonding difficulties between parent and child might be a result of the disorder rather than the cause.

Myth #4: Selectively mute children use their silence as a form of passive aggression, manipulation, or defiance.

Oppositional behavior may be in the eye of the beholder (or perhaps we should say, in the *ear* of the frustrated would-be listener), but taking this view of mutism implies a conscious choice of silence by the selectively mute child. If selective mutism does represent a speech phobia, it is not surprising that these children appear to

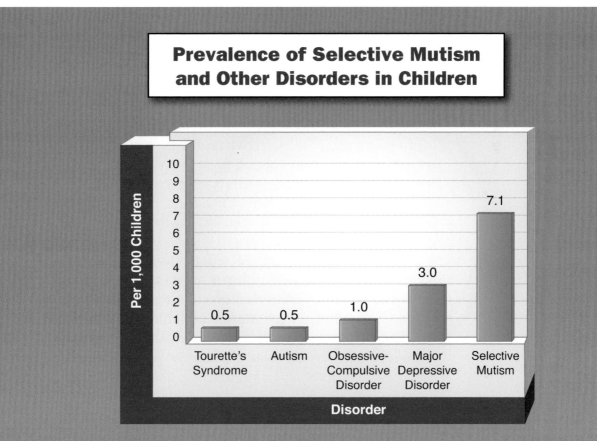

Prevalence of Selective Mutism and Other Disorders in Children

Taken from: www.selectivemutism.org.

stubbornly resist attempts to make them speak, just as, for example, a person with a fear of flying would not willingly board an airplane.

Additionally, it is wise to remember that power struggles between adults and children are no-win situations and the only winning strategy is to avoid them. One might ask who is being more oppositional, the child who is afraid to speak or the adult who stubbornly insists that the child must speak.

Appropriate Interventions

Myth #5: Selective mutism is extremely difficult to treat.

Historically this may have been true, but when treatment is approached with an understanding of selective mutism as an anxiety disorder, most children make excellent progress. Anecdotal evidence does suggest, however, that early diagnosis and multimodal treatment is critical for the greatest chance of successful treatment outcome.

Myth #6: Selective mutism is really just severe shyness; most children will grow out of it.

Shyness is a non-pathologic personality trait but it is not paralyzing, as is selective mutism. The inability to speak when speech is expected leads to severe incapacitation, inability to perform well in school without special accommodations, and poor self-esteem because of the frustration and anger reflected by teachers, peers, and others.

Although a percentage of selectively mute children apparently do overcome mutism without formal intervention, anecdotal reports indicate that these individuals continue to suffer from other manifestations of anxiety. And, since there is no way to identify which children may "outgrow" it, physicians and educators should recommend evaluation of any child meeting the DSM-IV [*Diagnostic and Statistical Manual of Mental Disorders, 4th ed.*] criteria for selective mutism for one month or more.

Otherwise, the window of opportunity for optimal treatment results will be missed in many cases.

One of the greatest frustrations for parents of selectively mute children is that if they seek advice of a pediatrician for a young child not speaking outside the home, they are usually told that their child is just shy, and then at the onset of kindergarten they are informed by school officials that the child is severely disturbed and needs psychological help.

Myth #7: Adults who work with selectively mute children should let the children know that there is a firm expectation for speech.

The expectation of speech is a trigger of severe, paralyzing anxiety for selectively mute children. Instead of embracing the simplistic notion that mutism will stop when reinforcers are removed, teachers, parents and therapists must understand that these children need interventions to reduce anxiety, as well as instruction on recognizing and coping with their anxious feelings before any speaking goals are placed on them. Allowing children to communicate non-verbally does not prolong mutism but actually serves to increase the child's comfort level (as well as allowing the child to have his or her basic needs met during the period before they are able to speak). It should be noted that many mute children do not need external motivation to speak; they simply need supportive, encouraging attitudes so they can discover that they can begin speaking in situations where they previously felt paralyzed by anxiety. . . .

FAST FACT

Many children with selective mutism respond well to very low doses of antidepressants.

Trapped in Silence

In summary, the lack of knowledge about selective mutism is a serious barrier to helping these children, but the incorrect ideas discussed here are even more damaging.

Teachers must be given adequate training about mutism and get advice from informed school administrators and psychologists to help identify children who may have selective mutism. (© Ellen B. Senisi/Photo Researchers, Inc.)

Selectively mute children have the best chance of overcoming their disability when there is an alliance between parents, teachers and therapists; currently, though, parents must risk false accusations of abuse, possibility of misdiagnosis, and inaccurate and misleading advice on how to help their children. One of the great tragedies for these families is that not only are the children trapped in silence, but the parents' voices are also stifled. Despite the fact that schools and therapists often do not know how to treat selectively mute children successfully, there is often too little attention paid to parental knowledge and instinct about their children.

Teachers also tend to be caught in the middle, with inadequate training about this disorder and the advice of well meaning but misinformed school administrators and psychologists to maintain firm expectations for the children to speak.

Fortunately there has been a shift in more recent publications, and several current authors do stress that selective mutism most likely has a biological basis rooted in anxiety. While there is agreement that more research is needed to substantiate the neurobiological and possibly genetic factors, there are already a number of reasons to favor this newer conceptualization over the older theories. Most notably, selectively mute children treated from the anxiety perspective (using protocols based on behavioral therapy and/or pharmacological treatments for anxiety) appear to be more likely to recover or make significant progress in overcoming selective mutism, when compared with case reports in the older literature of children whose therapy was more dynamic and psychoanalytic in nature. As more people are educated about the recent and ongoing research about selective mutism, there is hope that the myths will yield to scientific knowledge and these children will be freed from their walls of silence.

CHAPTER 3

Living with Speech Disorders

Love Beyond Words: Parenting a Daughter with Severe Speech Impairments

Robert Rummel-Hudson

In the following selection Robert Rummel-Hudson describes some of his day-to-day experiences as the father of a young girl with a brain disorder that impairs her ability to speak. His daughter, Schuyler, uses a portable communication device with a screen and word keys to express herself audibly. The author shares some of Schuyler's breakthroughs—such as when she first consciously recognized that she was unable to talk—and the many challenges of living in a world that often misunderstands or fears people with disabilities.

Rummel-Hudson is the author of *Schuyler's Monster: A Father's Journey with His Wordless Daughter.*

When his daughter, Schuyler, was 18 months old, a simple question from a pediatrician ("Is she making any effort to speak?") transformed Robert Rummel-Hudson from befuddled new dad into the last thing any father or mother ever expects or desires to be-

Photo on facing page. Parents with children who suffer from speech disorders have a daily battle to help their children communicate. (© **Lea Paterson/Photo Researchers, Inc.**)

come: a special-needs parent. Eventually Schuyler was diagnosed, at age 3, with polymicrogyria—a rare brain malformation that can result in symptoms ranging from problems swallowing to grand mal seizures and varying levels of retardation. In Schuyler's case, it has affected her ability to articulate words. For several years, Rummel-Hudson has blogged about his journey with his daughter, who now attends school and communicates with the help of a computerized box she carries with her. "When the doctor gave us the diagnosis, it was as if the bushes parted and out stepped a monster," he recalls. "The dreadful thing in Schuyler's head had a name." While fighting his own depression and the nagging sense that he was not the right person for the job, he became an advocate to help his child cope with her disability. Here are posts from Rummel-Hudson's ongoing blog (www.schuylersmonsterblog.com).

Eighty-Four Keys

January 14, 2007. We had our monthly parents meeting last night at Schuyler's school. It's always an interesting and humbling experience for Julie (Schuyler's mom) and me to spend time with other special-needs parents. It serves as a reminder that most of them—well, all of them, actually—have tenacious and smart kids who, in their individual ways, are nevertheless either slightly or significantly worse off than our daughter. Schuyler is the luckiest of unlucky kids.

Before the meeting began, the two members of Schuyler's Assistive Technology team who have been working with her from the beginning pulled us aside. They told us they think Schuyler is ready to move up to the next level on her Alternative Augmented Communication (AAC) device—a portable touch screen with programmed word keys that allows her to express herself and respond to questions audibly. "She needs more words," they said.

Schuyler's speech device is currently set to display 45 keys at a time. This new setting will bring it up to 84 keys, which is the maximum on her device, known hereabouts as her Big Box of Words (BBoW). Schuyler will be using the same setting as adults who use this device.

Well, I can't begin to tell you how happy we are—happy and proud and, most of all, vindicated. When she attended her little Austin [Texas]–area elementary school two years ago, the district insisted it was unlikely Schuyler would be capable of using this advanced device. Although they never said so, Julie and I always suspected the reason they kept lowballing her had as much to do with budget constraints as anything else. Updating Schuyler's device would cost thousands of dollars.

Rather than admit that or deal with the funding issue head-on, they claimed Schuyler was incapable of using the BBoW at all. ("Not educationally necessary" was the phrase I remember most vividly.) Not even two years later, she's moving up to the most advanced setting. It's worth saying again (and if you're a parent out there with misgivings about what your kid's teachers are telling you, I hope you're listening): *They were wrong, and we were right.*

If we'd stopped fighting that fight, Schuyler would still be sitting in a cramped little special-ed class, trying to teach sign language to her teachers who didn't know it. She wouldn't be educated, so much as taken care of, and when she reached the age of 17, she would leave them, not as a high school graduate but rather as Not Their Problem.

Instead, she's in first grade, doing the same work and taking the same tests and obsessing over the same Hello Kitty merchandise as all the other 7-year-olds.

Underestimating Schuyler will bite you on the rear every single time. It's becoming clear that she might just be the smartest one of us all.

Mermaids

January 20, 2007. We were at Target today, buying clothes for Schuyler. As we wandered the store, we ended up in

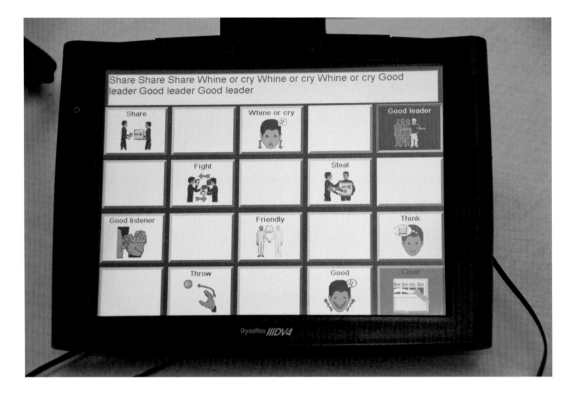

Alternative and augmented communication devices are portable touch screens with programmed word keys that allow children with speech disorders to express themselves and respond to questions audibly. (© Ellen B. Senisi/Photo Researchers, Inc.)

the DVD section, where Schuyler spotted *The Little Mermaid.* We realized she had only seen the crappy TV-series version, never the movie itself, so her mom and I got it for her, because we're swell.

It's definitely been a few years since I'd seen *The Little Mermaid,* long enough that I'd forgotten the deal that Ariel makes with Ursula, the giant, squid-legged drag queen, to give up her voice in exchange for some legs.

Schuyler was already captivated by all the mermaids, but when Ariel's voice was taken away, something occurred to Schuyler—something she's never actually come out and addressed with us. For the first time in her life, Schuyler *told* us that she can't talk.

She pointed to the TV and then pointed into her open mouth while shaking her head. She then gestured to just herself, again shaking her head. "I don't talk," she said over and over again in her strange, no-consonant language that we can usually understand but which is pretty much Martian to the rest of the world.

Later, when Ariel got her voice back, Schuyler turned and looked at us with an unreadable expression. But after the movie, she clearly wanted to discuss the issue further, and continued to tell us with gestures that, like Ariel, she had no voice.

When her mom reminded her that she had her BBoW to speak for her, Schuyler very carefully searched for just the right words, typing out "no mouth" at first, but frowning and deleting her unsatisfactory choice. I don't think she knew exactly what she wanted to say, only that she saw something that resonated with her own life, and wanted us to understand.

I feel a heavy sadness about the evening, the same way I do every time Schuyler faces a harsh reality. Still, I can't help but think that something really important and positive happened tonight, even if it was accidental. That's usually how Schuyler's big moments happen. They sneak upon us, and leave us pondering long after Schuyler has grabbed the evening's carefully chosen dolls and climbed the ladder to her bed.

I can only imagine what she dreams about. Perhaps she speaks in her dreams, as she does in mine.

Coffee Talk

April 8, 2007. Sometimes we do things for Schuyler that help her along in the world. We make decisions and sacrifices that turn out to be the right ones and which propel her down smooth, bright roads.

Most of the time, however, she pushes herself down those roads.

The other day, we took Schuyler to a huge play area at a semi-fancy local mall so she could run around and play without being subjected to (or subjecting her parents to) fried "foods," cheap Happy Meal toys, or demented clowns. It was one of those new trendy playgrounds made of squishy giant forms that the kids can climb around on and fall off of without incurring litigation.

At this particular play area, the theme was "giant breakfast." A 20-foot plate held a steak the size of a mattress along with two wagon wheel-size eggs. A slice of grapefruit was topped with a cherry as large as a basketball.

It is a very cool playground.

Schuyler was having her usual great time on the Big Breakfast: I think it's probably her favorite place to play, with the possible exception of the oft-requested Clown House o' Happy Meals. It wasn't long before she'd made some friends. In this case, it was two sisters who wanted to run around the giant plate, alternately chasing and being chased by Schuyler, and their brother, who kept up as best he could despite a cast on one leg. After exhausting themselves, the four of them climbed into the giant, Jacuzzi-size coffee cup and began the whole "So who are you and what's your scene?" discussion. Before it got very far, Schuyler ran over to us and grabbed her BBoW.

What happened next stopped us in our tracks. And by "us" I don't mean just Julie and me.

As Schuyler began demonstrating her device and asking questions of all the kids present, the adults watched in wonder. Four, then six, then eight kids crowded around the giant cup, fascinated by this hard-playing, hard-laughing little girl with the robot voice. I think the grown-ups worried about the Revolution of the Small beginning at that moment.

At the center of it all was Schuyler. She asked everyone their names and how old they were, and she answered their questions as best she could. She led a cyborgian rendition of "Old MacDonald Had a Farm." And when one little girl repeatedly tried to reach over and take the BBoW, Schuyler told her "No" and sternly pointed at the ground outside the cup until the little girl glumly climbed out and skulked away.

Banished by the Cyborg Princess. It's a harsh world in Schuyler's Coffee Cup.

For a full 20 minutes, Schuyler held court. I could see at a glance that while the kids were all fascinated by and even envious of Schuyler and the BBoW, their moms were a little freaked out.

That's how it usually happens. If someone gets spooked by Schuyler or her monster it's almost always another adult, as if their kid might catch whatever she has. Kids her age tend to absorb what's different, make quick adjustments in order to facilitate play, and then go on.

Can't talk? Well then, let's run around and howl instead. . . .

Rough Transition

June 5, 2007. Schuyler had a bad day at her summer program. She has an incident like this about once a year, which is probably not too bad for a soon-to-be 8-year-old.

Today she got frustrated and kicked a kid in her class, and then one of the adults as well. I'm still not sure we've gotten the whole story, but she admitted to the kicking on her BBoW. She said the boy hurt her first, but she didn't have an explanation for kicking the staffer. She shrugged miserably when we asked her why she did it, because I don't think she understands having a temper, or how to respond to her own frustration.

It's a particular difficulty with nonverbal kids, especially when they are interacting with new people who don't understand how to communicate with them. That doesn't excuse Schuyler's behavior, but this sort of thing doesn't just occur in a vacuum. The BBoW requires patience from everyone, since it takes her some time to respond to questions or express what she's feeling.

Well, it's only the second day.

She promised to apologize on her device to the people she kicked and to be the very best little girl she can be tomorrow, and I believe she'll do just that. After our

> **FAST FACT**
>
> In polymicrogyria, the brain develops too many folds, and the folds are unusually small. Its symptoms vary depending on how much of the brain is affected.

long talk and mutual agreement on her punishment this evening—no TV—and what would happen tomorrow if things don't improve, she looked at me sadly and started punching buttons on her device.

"I love you," she said.

"I love you, too, Schuyler," I said. "I love you so, so much."

She smiled for the first time all evening and climbed out of her chair. She came over and put her arms around my neck and hugged me as hard as she's ever hugged me, and for a long time.

Future Girl

June 12, 2007. For the past few days. I've been listening to the audiobook of Anne Lamott's *Plan B: Further Thoughts on Faith.* I'm a big fan of Lamott, even if we've arrived at different places spiritually, and I was a fan even before we had Schuyler or met the monster. A passage from the chapter called "Diamondheart" jumped out at me. Lamott writes about her son, Sam:

"I can see myself so clearly in him, many of my worst traits, some of my goodness. I can also still see many of Sam's ages in him: New parents always grieve as their babies get bigger, because they cannot imagine the child will ever be so heartbreakingly cute and needy again. But Sam is a swirl of every age he's ever been, and all the new ones, like cotton candy, like the Milky Way."

When I heard that, I realized that the same is true of Schuyler, and no doubt of every other kid as well. When I look at her, I can see the newborn she was, back when she was fat as a slug and covered with strange black hair, like a baby Wookiee. I can see her as a stumbling toddler, her body already starting to lengthen, her transition from baby to girl beginning, yet with those fat cheeks remaining. When I look at Schuyler, who has become a rambunctious, leggy tornado of a girl, I can see the baby I wore against my chest, shortly after moving to Connecticut, shielding her impossibly tiny body from the bitter cold blowing in from the Long Island Sound. She remains all those Schuylers to me.

Some moments I can even see into the future. I can see, like ghost images in a photo in which the subject moves too fast for the shutter speed, the shadow of a pretty teenager who speaks like a robot but still makes that face at boys and causes them, and me, heartbreak and despair. When we're out these days, I sometimes see teenage girls who are embarrassed by their fathers, and others who still cling to them unashamedly, and I suspect Schuyler will be a little of both. I can see her a decade from now, still dressing against the norms of the elite girls of North Dallas, where we live now, yet maintaining her outsider "cred"—the oddball stunner who carries her cyborg voice in a stylish bag and doesn't wait to be told how to be cool. Sometimes I can even see Schuyler the young woman, the one who'll go to college or go out into the world and make a place for herself on her own terms. In my most selfish dreams, Schuyler the young woman will be a writer, and she'll pick up the thread of chronicling her amazing and unpredictable life after I am no longer around to contribute.

Of course, I can't divine what Schuyler's life will really be like. I can't even begin. But sometimes she'll look into me with those eyes, the eyes of a child wise beyond her years. When she does, I can see the person she'll grow up to be, the wild and broken and astonishing and perfect woman she was born to become. Schuyler looks more and more like her mother as she grows older, but I see so much of myself in those eyes, and in that crooked smile she flashes right before she does something that causes everyone in the room to hurriedly say, "No! Nononon-ononono! Give me that! . . ."

When people ask what I do, I tell them I'm a writer. But the truth is, I am Schuyler's father, her launchpad, and when I reach the end my days, I hope she'll be standing there beside me to send me on my way.

The Psychological Terror of Stuttering

Ed Arrington

Attempting to communicate with a severe stutter is emotionally devastating, writes Ed Arrington in the following selection. The humiliation and shame that stuttering causes damages one's sense of self-worth and self-esteem, says Arrington. This shame can also lead to isolation and loneliness, as it did for a time in the author's life.

Arrington is a former US Air Force clerk who now lives in Jacksonville, Florida.

M any years ago when I was in the Air Force, stationed in San Antonio, Texas, I went through a traumatic, distressing, and humiliating experience.

I worked as a clerk in an office, and it was my job (among other clerical duties) to answer all incoming phone calls. I received a routine call one day. The only other person in the office was an Army Major, a kind man. My telephone conversation that day was brief—I said hello, identified myself and the office I worked in and then listened for the reply. I was asked to comment on a particular subject—but sadly I was unable to comply with the request.

I was in psychological terror, because I stuttered very badly on a daily basis.

I eventually just hung up the phone and lowered my head in embarrassment and shame—welcome to the world of one who stutters.

A Heartless Enemy

I'm not going to give you a medical definition of stuttering (and there are some)—It's a malady that anyone can spot. Scientists don't know why people stutter. Boys are 3 times more likely than girls to suffer from this. About 1% of adults are affected by it. 1% is a big percentage for me, however, because I am prone to stutter anytime, and when it happens, it's like twisting a knife through my stomach, shredding precious organs. That picture translated to stuttering means my self-esteem and self-worth have just been pulverized. I've become aware that a heartless enemy is trying again to bring me down.

For a long time, stuttering made a major impact on my social life. I would shy away from group settings because I could not be sure I would not stutter. I recall vividly during Basic Training in the Air Force the time I stood before an instructor and stuttered so bad that he, in pity, frustration, and perhaps, scorn, dismissed me from his presence—I really don't think the poor man knew what to do—in retrospect, it would be easy to feel sympathy for him. I recall the time in church when someone asked me to pray in a class. Because I could not get the words out I stopped and requested someone else pray. I did not go back to church for a long time after that.

> **FAST FACT**
>
> Often, people who stutter try to do something to "fix" their speech. They may tense their muscles, tap their foot, or blink their eyes in an effort to push the words out.

Still an Impact

Professional Therapy has suggested there are cures for stuttering. There's an anti-stuttering device—also a 12 day Therapy course, and many others.

I haven't used any of these—I've just worked hard to control it and especially not use too many words in any conversation that involve "S"'s or "T"'s. On the in-frequent occasion that I might stutter now, it's hard to make myself think "Hey, I've really improved, I haven't stuttered in a long time"—remember that knife in my stomach? The impact will always be deadly and heartless, plunging me for a time into abject misery.

Finally, I think back to that kind Army major in my office. He heard every labored attempt to speak that day. After I hung up the phone, he walked over and placed his hand on my shoulder. He ultimately helped me find a speech therapist. That was not a cure, but it was the important first step toward mastering the struggle with stuttering. That itself has proved to be a wonderful ben-efit, and because of it, I am determined to not ever fall to the heartless malady of "stuttering."

Confessions of a Covert Stutterer

Cathy O.

The following piece is written by Cathy O., a resident of Ferndale, Michigan, who works in the human resources department at the Ford Motor Company. Cathy coleads the Royal Oak Chapter of the National Stuttering Association and the Dearborn Kids/Teens Who Stutter Chapter. Here she shares what it is like to be a covert stutterer. She may sound fluent to those who hear her, but she often rephrases her thoughts, substitutes words, and engages in other tricks to avoid the sounds that she tends to stutter. While she does not usually tell people that she stutters, she has become more accepting of her disorder through support from the National Stuttering Association.

My name is Cathy, but I sometimes go by Anne because it's easier to say. I am a covert person who stutters (PWS) and will do all I can to avoid stuttering. I sometimes change my name in situations where I will never meet or see that person again (i.e. calling for information, dinner reservations, casually chatting with a stranger). Up until five years ago, I would use "Anne" quite often to avoid stuttering. I still change my name at times based on the circumstance, but not as often as I used to.

This is all due to the National Stuttering Association (NSA), a support organization for people who stutter in the United States. Since my initial involvement over ten years ago, I have slowly accepted myself as a PWS. Do I like it? Heck no, but I have learned to live with it and not to let it upset me as much as before.

Covert Actions

Some of the other crazy things I have done to hide my stuttering are: record over parts of home movies that show me stuttering as a kid; holding my hand up like a glove and pointing to the lower right when someone asks me where I am from (being from Michigan, I can do that); spending countless hours practicing saying my name out loud when preparing for a meeting; rerecording a message on someone's voicemail dozens of times until it is perfect; changing what city I live in; having nicknames for many of my friends if I can't say their name; developing acronyms and "cool names" for places we go (i.e. I call 'Starbucks' 'S Bucks'); using the mailing address of our chapter leader as my address to receive NSA publications so my roommates would not find out that I stutter; never returning books to the library 20 years ago because they changed it to a manual drop-off and I didn't want someone to know that I checked out books on stuttering.

Journey Toward Acceptance

My journey toward acceptance of my stuttering began when I was 26 years old, which was the first time I talked to anyone about my stuttering. Most of my life I wouldn't even say or write the word *stutter* because of all the pain associated with it—I referred to it as "the S word". One day I was having a tough time at work making phone calls, so I searched the Internet for information on stuttering. I discovered that there was an organization for people who stutter—the NSA—and a local support group chapter in my area. I printed out all the materials, even the information about the local meetings, but then hid it somewhere in my house where no one could find it. Months went by, when a person told me about his friend's daughter who stutters and how she was having a hard time. So, I made copies, gave them to him to give to her and Voila . . . we decided to attend a support group meeting together.

The first time I attended these meetings I did not feel like I fit in. Everyone was stuttering openly, some worse than others. I could not find anyone there who talked like me but yet, I could not find anyone outside of that room that talked like me either. It made me wonder if I really did stutter. Then the next day as I went to answer my phone, I realized that my stutter is real. I continued to go to the meetings and slowly realized how much they helped me and that I was not alone. It wasn't until about two years later that anyone in the group actually heard me stutter. It took me that long to even let a small repetition be heard. To me, it is more exhausting pushing through my stutter than hiding it.

After attending the support group meetings for a year, I decided to attend the annual NSA conference with other chapter members. I was amazed by everything I experienced—workshops, ceremonies, keynote speakers, the children's activities, and just hanging out with other people who stutter. I couldn't believe a place like that existed, where people who stuttered were the majority. But still, I didn't feel like I belonged. I was asked many times "are you an SLP [speech-language pathologist]?" because I was totally fluent. I would not let my guard down, even in that environment. I felt like I didn't stutter enough to fit in the stuttering world but was too disfluent to fit into the "real world". It was like I was on an elevator caught between two floors and I was stuck all alone.

A Breakthrough

Shortly before attending my second national conference I was asked to be a panelist on the first ever Covert Stuttering Workshop, which now has been going strong for eight years! I unenthusiastically agreed. While giving my presentation I was as smooth as can be the whole way through, until I got stuck on a word I could not change. I started to say it, I stopped, started again while beginning to stutter, stopped—this went on for what felt like an hour but was actually two minutes. I tried to write the word on the board but the audience would not let me get away with that. With the audience screaming, "just say it" over and over again, I just said it—N-N-N-N-N-N-N-N-NATURAL. That was the end of my presentation as I was so embarrassed. But it was the beginning of my becoming more open about my stuttering because everyone finally heard me stutter for the first time and I actually felt like they truly knew I belonged there.

After this HUGE breakthrough, I spent many hours becoming more involved in the NSA, more time getting to know my friends who stuttered, pushed myself a little bit more out of my comfort zone, but still . . . I was so fearful of anyone hearing me stutter. I allowed my stuttering to continue to be in the forefront of every thought, conversation and situation. I was frustrated as I watched others become more accepting of their stuttering but after three plus years of attending support group meetings, I still fought it with all I had.

One of my turning points and most shameful incidents that made me realize I needed to stop putting so much extra time into hiding my stutter happened about six years ago. My grandmother was put into hospice and on that same day, my step-dad was involved in a horrible car accident which put him in a coma for over two

weeks. I knew I had to call my boss to let her know that I would not be at work the next day. I needed to be there for my mom. I waited until late at night so I would get my boss's voicemail and no one was around to hear me make the call. The entire process took me well over an hour. I spent several minutes writing down what I wanted to say, calling my voicemail to practice, replaying the message, rewriting what I wanted to say, calling back again to practice—over and over again. When I was ready, I called my boss's voicemail left a message, listened to it, rerecorded it, listened to it again, rerecorded it over and over until I got it just right.

Here I was, worried about my speech when two members of my immediate family were barely alive. This is when I realized I had to stop wasting so much time trying to sound perfectly fluent and I had to stop letting my stutter control my life so much.

After attending support groups like this one for a year, Cathy attended the NSA conference, where workshops, ceremonies, keynote speakers, and children's activities allow stutterers to relate to people with the same speech disorder. (© **Gerald Herbert/The Washington Times/Landov**)

Avoidance Techniques

Some say that stuttering is stuttering and overt and covert are all the same—if you stutter, you stutter. While many of the traits, behaviors and feelings are the same, I disagree on some levels. Many PWS have told me they can be covert by avoiding a situation or just not talking. But to me, that is not what defines being covert.

Being covert means that when faced with the situation I can usually get my point across and talk fluently without the listener suspecting I stutter. This is achieved by much word substitution, rephrasing, an occasional little cough or sneeze somewhere mid sentence or an "I forgot" and a few minutes later an "ah, I remember now!" when I feel I can say what I want to say fluently, and several other tricks and techniques I have developed over my lifetime of avoiding. True, I do hear pauses here and there, and breathing mid-sentence when listening to a voicemail I may leave someone, but I truly believe that most would not peg me as someone who stutters.

When someone tells me 'just stutter', it does not work for me. I do tend to say what I want more often now and a stutter may slip out here and there. I may have an experience where I say my name horribly and although I still feel embarrassed and ashamed in the moment, I don't carry that feeling with me all day as I did before. I deal better with the negative emotions but my actions are usually the same—to try to avoid stuttering all together. I can practice my name alone for hours and be fine but in the situation, something takes over and I have no control. If I stuttered badly while introducing myself to this person or in this situation so I believe I will do so again. It's like I associate my name with stuttering and that takes precedence over all the mental work I did to prepare for that moment.

FAST FACT

Severe stutterers cannot mask their disorder. Covert stutterers are mostly people whose stutter is either mild or moderate.

Habits Are Hard to Break

Over the years, friends have found out I stutter thanks to the Internet (they have 'Googled' me and find out that I stutter by the various articles I have written and of my involvement with the NSA). When I ask them if they were aware that I stutter, only one said they knew, a couple said they never knew and a few said they thought I just talked differently but that they wouldn't label me as a PWS. Even though these few know that I stutter, I still try my best to hide it when speaking with them. Just because "my secret" is out of the bag with them, I do not let the stutter out of the bag too often. The shame and embarrassment has been embedded in me and although that has become a little less of an issue, I feel I will always try to hide my stuttering in someway. Habits are hard to break.

However, it is nice to talk to these friends who now know I stutter and be honest about where I am going. For so long, (and I still do this with those who do not know that I stutter) every time I went to an NSA meeting or event, I would tell people I was visiting with friends or at a work event.

I do not advertise that I stutter, talk about it with friends, family, coworkers or others I encounter because for so long, it has been hidden. How do you all of a sudden let this secret out of the bag? Hiding my stuttering has been such a big part of my life—a daily occurrence—that if it becomes visible, will I still be the same person in people's eyes?

I have become more accepting of my stutter because of the unconditional love and support from the NSA and all the great people I have met who also stutter. Some of my best friends are people who stutter. There is a special bond we have, this commonality (stuttering) that is unique. It has been a long journey indeed, and I have a ways to go but it is nice knowing I have so many by my side who can relate to the real me—a person who stutters.

When the Words Started to Disappear

Kim O'Connell

In the following selection Kim O'Connell examines selective mutism (SM) and shares what it is like to mother a son with this disorder. Initially believing that her son, Declan, was simply introverted, O'Connell noticed that there were longer and longer periods of time during which he could not speak. Declan's mutism began during a time of transition—just after beginning preschool and before the birth of his baby sister. Therapy with a psychologist and specialist in childhood anxiety and SM has helped him to resume talking, although he remains mute at school.

Based in Arlington, Virginia, Kim O'Connell blogs about selective mutism and parenting sensitive children at www.bloomingboy.com.

"There's tape in my belly and all the words are stuck there," my son Declan said to me, after another long day of complete silence. His words had come forth in a rush, like a flash flood in a slot canyon. Quickly, I tried to understand what he was experiencing, to keep him talking, to stave off that mysterious force that would make the words disappear again. I knew it was only a matter of time.

At the age of three, my son was diagnosed with selective mutism (SM), a rare anxiety disorder in which people speak comfortably in some places or with some people and are struck utterly mute in other situations. For parents, it is a sad, confounding, and frustrating condition. Many times I felt so desperate to hear my son's voice that I wanted to pry his mouth open and pull the words out myself. For children, SM can be painfully debilitating and can hinder their ability to advance in school, make friends, and participate in activities. If left untreated, it can lead to adult anxiety and depression. And in one notorious case, SM may even have contributed to a heinous act of mass violence.

A Misunderstood Disorder

SM is recognized by the American Psychiatric Association as a real mental disorder often associated with social phobia. Despite this fact, teachers, pediatricians, and other people too often dismiss this affliction as mere shyness. "He'll grow out of it," we've been told. "My kid was shy too and he's fine." Dr. Elisa Shipon-Blum, a nationally recognized expert on SM, has written that the disorder is "the *most* misdiagnosed, mismanaged, and mistreated anxiety disorder of childhood. Children with selective mutism truly suffer in silence, and yet most people completely misunderstand the child's silence." This patronizing attitude can deprive mute children of the therapy or medication—and even just the empathy—that SM requires.

Declan has always had a reserved temperament. As a toddler, he was never one to perform for strangers, refusing to say "hi" or "thank you" or wave bye-bye on command. I once hosted a playgroup in my small basement, parents and children jumbled together like rag dolls in a trunk, and it took a while for me to notice that Declan had disappeared. I found him alone in his bedroom, curled up on the floor. "I like it better by myself," he said. As an introvert, too, I thought little of it at the time.

Then his words started to disappear.

Longer and Longer Silences

It was a period of transition: Declan had started preschool, I was pregnant, we were preparing to move. He stopped talking first to his teachers and classmates, then to his nanny and extended family, and then, terrifyingly, to my husband and me. The periods of mutism lasted longer each time, from one hour to four hours and then 36 hours and longer, while the periods of speech shrank. At one point, Declan didn't say a word to anyone for nearly two weeks straight. At the time, record snowfalls were blanketing the Washington, D.C., area where we live. Our house was suddenly unbearably quiet, like the world outside our door. I went nearly mad trying to force my son to talk.

In those rare moments when he was verbal, Declan's self-awareness was achingly beautiful. "I feel like the words are locked behind a door," he once said, "and I don't have the key." When he was mute, I would ask him where the words were, and he would usually point to his feet. If they were up to his belly, it was a good day. They were never near his mouth.

Learning About Selective Mutism

As an antidote to my anxiety, I educated myself about selective mutism. I learned that SM is usually diagnosed during the preschool years, when children face the first real performance pressure of their lives. I learned that the condition was once called "elective mutism," as if children were being willfully defiant with their silence. The psychiatric profession changed the name in 1994 to reflect its current understanding that mutism is actually an involuntary anxious response. I learned that, while SM is not on the autism spectrum, the one is often confused with the other, and behaviors and treatments can be similar. I even found a little ditty about SM written by Sir Paul McCartney, that goes partly like this:

FAST FACT

Most children with selective mutism have a genetic predisposition to anxiety.

She's given up talking
Don't say a word
Even in the classroom
Not a dickie bird

What disturbed me most, however, was the story of Seung-Hui Cho, who killed 32 people and wounded 25 others at Virginia Tech in April 2007. Along with schizophrenia and depression, Cho suffered from selective mutism. He was treated with medication and therapy but apparently never cured. On his dormitory wall, he had written telling lyrics from the song "Shine" by the band Collective Soul: "Teach me how to speak, teach me how to share." He ultimately made his voice known in the most gruesome way possible.

Our son will not have that same fate—not if I can help it. Our pediatrician referred us to a wonderful psychologist who specializes in childhood anxiety and SM. Through therapy, and by changing our parenting style and removing all pressure on Declan to speak, things have improved. Declan's words have returned in stages. He resumed talking to us at home, and then to friends on play dates, and eventually to his nanny. With the help of his caring teachers, he's gotten more and more comfortable at school, too, although he's still not verbal there.

On the bright spring day I gave birth to our baby daughter—a day so weighted, so fraught with change that I was sure Declan would lose his words again—I was relieved to hear from my in-laws at home that he was still talking. When my husband brought him to visit me in the hospital, he loudly said, "Where's the baby?" I exhaled.

But we have a long way to go. Declan is still mute in school. He still has a lot of anxiety, more than any four-year-old should. And I still have a hard time getting people to understand that selective mutism is much more than shyness. But I'll keep talking about it. I am finding my voice, just as Declan is finding his.

GLOSSARY

aphasia	Total or partial loss of the ability to use or understand language, usually caused by stroke, brain disease, or injury.
apraxia	A speech disorder in which voluntary muscle movement is impaired without muscle weakness. Apraxia may be acquired or developmental, with differing degrees of severity. Also known as dyspraxia.
articulation	The touching of one movable structure (such as the tongue) to another surface (such as the teeth) to form words.
articulation disorder	A type of speech disorder characterized by the way sounds are formed.
cluttering	The rapid repetition or production of speech sounds occurring without awareness on the part of the speaker.
communication disorder	Any disorder characterized by an impaired ability to communicate, including language, speech, and hearing disorders.
covert stuttering	The persistent attempts to hide one's stuttering by substituting words or rearranging phrases to avoid the words that are difficult to speak.
dysarthria	Speech disorder caused by a weakness or lack of coordination of the speech muscles, usually resulting from brain or neural damage.
dysfluency	Any break or interruption in speech.
dysphonia	Any impairment of the voice or speaking ability.
language disorder	Communication disorder characterized by an impaired ability to understand or use words in their proper context.

larynx	The organ in the throat involved in breathing and sound production. Often referred to as the "voice box," the larynx contains the vocal folds that produce voice.
lisp	An articulation error in which one substitutes one speech sound for another, such as using *th* instead of *s* in the word *yes*.
phonological disorder	A speech disorder seen in those who have difficulty learning and organizing how sounds work together to create words.
phonology	The science of speech sounds and sound patterns.
selective mutism	A condition in which children feel anxious and inhibited and cannot speak in certain situations.
speech disorder	Communication disorder characterized by an impaired ability to produce speech sounds or by problems with voice quality.
speech-language pathologist	This career field, also known as a speech therapist, is concerned with disorders of speech and language.
stuttering	Speech disorder in which speech has more dysfluencies than is considered average.
vocal cords/folds	Either of the two pairs of folds of mucous membrane located in the throat and projecting into the cavity of the larynx that vibrate at different rates to produce voice.

CHRONOLOGY

B.C.	600	Aesop, the creator of fables, is said to have had a speech disorder.
	384–322	The Greek orator and statesman Demosthenes practiced speaking with pebbles in his mouth to overcome his stuttering.
A.D.	c. 120	The Greek physician Soranus of Ephesus differentiates between speech disorders caused by tongue paralysis and those rooted in other causes.
	c. 500	The Roman physician and author Caelius Aurelianus distinguishes problems of voice from problems of speech.
	c. 1300–1368	French surgeon Guy de Chauliac ascribes stuttering to excessive moisture or dryness of the tongue or brain.
	1493–1541	Swiss alchemist Paracelsus discovers the relationship between head wounds and paralysis and observes that defects of speech could occur in the absence of paralysis.
	1530–1606	Hieronymus Mercurialis, a Greek and Latin scholar and physician, writes extensively about speech disorders. He defines stuttering as a "hesitation of the tongue" and saw the condition as one in which people were compelled to repeat the first syllable of words.
	1669	Swiss physician John Conrad Amman writes about how to instruct people who stutter.

PERSPECTIVES ON DISEASES AND DISORDERS

1700s European treatments for stuttering include cutting the tongue with scissors and cutting nerves and neck or lip muscles.

1770 German physician Johann Gesner writes *Die Sprachamnesie*, a major study of aphasia. In it, he profiles several patients, focusing on one, K.D., who exhibited symptoms of what Gesner calls "speech amnesia."

1773 John Herries, a lecturer who taught in Scotland and England, publishes *Treatise on the Elements of Speech*. He explores the physiology of the organs of speech, describes the mechanisms of speech production, and examines topics such as deafness and speech impediments.

1827 American medical scientist James Rush publishes *The Philosophy of the Human Voice*. It presents a scientific notation system for describing speech sounds. The book is influential among elocutionists and speech therapists of the nineteenth century.

1828 French physician Marc Colombat de l'Isere develops the muthonome, a mechanical spring device issuing beats to create a timed rhythm with which a stutterer could speak.

1841 US physician and professor of elocution Andrew Comstock publishes *A System of Elocution with Special Reference to Gesture, to the Treatment of Stammering and Defective Articulation*. Comstock also invents a phonetic alphabet to use for speech instruction. His treatments for stuttering include repeated sound drills based on the phonetic alphabet and the recitation of memorized passages aloud.

1860s French physician Paul Pierre Broca discovers that the speech production center in humans is located in the frontal lobe of the brain's left hemisphere.

1872   US inventor Alexander Graham Bell opens the School of Vocal Physiology in Boston, Massachusetts. The school's focus was on training for the deaf and improving the speech of stutterers and others with communication disabilities.

1874   Prussian neurologist Carl Wernicke discovers that aphasia can result from damage to an area on the left posterior part of the brain where the temporal lobe meets the parietal lobe.

1882   Physician and stutterer Samuel Potter, an Irish immigrant in America, writes *Speech and Its Defects: Considered Physiologically, Pathologically, Historically, and Remedially.* His general classification of speech impediments includes alalia (language and motor speech disorders arising from brain damage or paralysis), paralalia (articulation disorders), and dyslalia (stuttering).

1904   US neurologist Charles K. Mills publishes "Treatment of Aphasia by Training" in the *Journal of the American Medical Association.* His therapy for aphasia includes phonetic drills moving from sounds and sound groups to syllables and words.

1912   American physician and psychologist Edward Wheeler Scripture writes *Stuttering and Lisping.* He divides lisping—his term for articulation disorders—into four subtypes: negligent lisping, organic lisping, neurotic lisping, and cluttering.

1916   American laryngologist James Sonnett Greene founds the National Hospital for Speech Disorders, a free clinic, in New York City. He advocates group therapy for stuttering, believing anxiety to be the main cause of the disorder.

1920   US clinicians Margaret Gray Blanton and Smiley Blanton publish *Speech Training for Children,* a book for parents and teachers on fostering good speech in normal children and therapies for stuttering children and children with articulation disorders.

1924   American phonetician Sarah T. Barrows is hired by the newly formed Speech Department at the University of Iowa to teach phonetics and to supervise a speech clinic. She emphasizes auditory stimulation in speech therapy.

1925   The American Speech-Language-Hearing Association is founded.

1926   The American Academy of Speech Correction approves a constitution and describes the group's objective as raising "existing standards of practice among workers in the field of speech correction." It also defines unethical practices, such as guaranteeing cures and charging exorbitant fees.

1926   Australian actor and speech therapist Lionel Logue opens a speech-defect clinic in London. The Duke of York—the future King George VI—hires Logue for long-term treatment for his stuttering.

1928   Sara Stinchfield, the first person in the United States to receive a PhD in speech pathology, writes *The Psychology of Speech,* the first in a series of books on different types of speech problems.

1931   Psychology and speech professor Lee Edward Travis's book *Speech Pathology* presents clinical subtypes for articulation problems, phonation problems, stuttering, and aphasia. Travis is instrumental in establishing the speech-pathology program at the University of Iowa.

1935   Lionel Logue founds the British Speech Therapy Society.

1937   American psychiatrist Samuel Orton publishes *Reading, Writing, and Speech Problems in Children: A Presentation of Certain Types of Disorders in the Development of the Language Faculty.* Orton hypothesizes that language and reading disabilities stem from a lack of hemispheric dominance in specific areas of the brain.

1939   American educator Mildred McGinnis publishes *Aphasic Children: Identification and Education by the Association Method.* Her therapy for aphasia focuses on the association of sounds with written letters, as well as sensory and motor association.

1947   Malcolm Fraser founds the Stuttering Foundation of America.

1948   German neuropsychiatrist Kurt Goldstein's influential book *Language and Language Disturbances* presents years of research with aphasic patients.

1962   Language philosopher John Austin proposes Speech Act Theory, an approach to language development that emphasizes the instrumental use of language over syntax. This theory was to influence speech therapy in the 1970s and 1980s.

1988   The US National Institute on Deafness and Other Communication Disorders is established.

2010   Researchers identify three genes linked to stuttering. *The King's Speech,* a movie depicting the therapeutic relationship between speech therapist Lionel Logue and British monarch King George VI, wins four Academy Awards, including Best Picture.

ORGANIZATIONS TO CONTACT

The editors have compiled the following list of organizations concerned with the issues debated in this book. The descriptions are derived from materials provided by the organizations. All have publications or information available for interested readers. The list was compiled on the date of publication of the present volume; the information provided here may change. Be aware that many organizations take several weeks or longer to respond to inquiries, so allow as much time as possible.

American Speech-Language-Hearing Association (ASHA)
2200 Research Blvd., Rockville, MD 20850-5650
(800) 638-8255
fax: (301) 296-8580
website: www.asha.org

Founded in 1925, ASHA is the professional, scientific, and credentialing organization for over 145,000 members who are speech-language pathologists, audiologists, and speech-language-hearing scientists in the United States and around the world. Its mission is to support professionals in the field of speech, language, and hearing science and to advocate on behalf of people with communication and related disorders. ASHA also provides an archive of educational resources to the public on its website, including links to frequently asked questions on aphasia, apraxia, stuttering, and other speech disorders and related conditions.

Canadian Stuttering Association (CSA)
PO Box 3027, Sherwood Park, AB T8H 2T1 CANADA
(866) 840-2906
website: www.stutter.ca

The CSA is a national not-for-profit organization committed to offering an impartial forum for the sharing of information, to advocating for Canadians who stutter, and to promoting greater acceptance of people who stutter by educating the public about the condition of stuttering. Its website includes contact information for support groups for people who stutter and links to research summaries and essays about stuttering, including "Stuttering: A Listener's Guide" and "Leaving the Fear Behind."

Childhood Apraxia of Speech Association of North America (CASANA)
416 Lincoln Ave., 2nd Fl., Pittsburgh, PA 15209
(412) 343-7102
website: www.apraxia-kids.org

CASANA is a publicly funded nonprofit organization with the goal of strengthening support systems in the lives of children with apraxia. It provides multimedia information and educational resources on childhood apraxia of speech to families, speech-language pathologists, policy makers, and the public. CASANA's website features a searchable online library with links to numerous articles, including "Characteristics of Childhood Apraxia of Speech" and "Late Blooming or Language Problem?"

National Aphasia Association (NAA)
350 Seventh Ave., Ste. 902, New York, NY 10001
(212) 267-2814
fax: (212) 267-2812
e-mail: naa@aphasia.org
website: www.aphasia.org

The NAA is a nonprofit group that promotes public education, research, rehabilitation, and support services to assist people with aphasia and their friends and families. The NAA provides contact information for aphasia community groups in the United States and Canada. Information on therapies, research trials, and rehabilitation research is available at its website. Its online library also provides links to articles on aphasia, brain injury, and stroke from various newspapers, journals, and magazines.

National Institute of Neurological Disorders and Stroke (NINDS)
PO Box 5801, Bethesda, MD 20824
(800) 352-9424
(301) 496-5751
website: www.ninds.nih.gov

A branch of the National Institutes of Health, NINDS conducts, fosters, and guides research on the causes, prevention, diagnosis, and treatment of neurological disorders and stroke. It also provides grants to public and private institutions and individuals in fields related to its areas of interest. Included at the NINDS website is an A–Z index of disorders, with informative entries on aphasia, apraxia, and brain injury.

National Institute on Deafness and Other Communication Disorders (NIDCD)
National Institutes of Health
31 Center Dr., MSC 2320, Bethesda, MD 20892-2320
(800) 241-1044
TTY: (800) 241-1055
e-mail: nidcdinfo@nidcd.nih.gov
website: www.nidcd.nih.gov

A branch of the US Department of Health and Human Services' National Institutes of Health, the NIDCD is the federal institute that conducts and supports medical and scientific research on normal and disordered hearing, balance, smell, taste, voice, speech, and language. The NIDCD aims to improve the lives of the millions of people who have communication disorders through advocacy, education, training, and research. Its website maintains a topical "A–Z" index with links to articles and information on various voice, speech, and language disorders.

National Stuttering Association (NSA)
119 W. Fortieth St., 14th Fl., New York, NY 10018
(800) 937-8888
(212) 944-4050
fax: (212) 944-8244
e-mail: info@westutter.org
website: www.nsastutter.org

The goal of the nonprofit NSA is to bring hope and empowerment to children and adults who stutter, their families, and professionals through support, education, advocacy, and research. The NSA has established more than 125 local self-help support groups for people who stutter. It also sponsors workshops for parents and children designed to educate families, teachers, and speech therapists about early diagnosis and effective intervention strategies. The NSA publishes two newsletters: *Letting Go* (for people who stutter) and *Family Voices* (for children, teens, parents, and therapists).

Selective Mutism Foundation (SMF)
ATTN: Carolyn Miller, PO Box 13133, Sissonville, WV 25360
or ATTN: Sue Newman, PO Box 25972, Tamarac, FL 33320
website: www.selectivemutismfoundation.org

The mission of the SMF is to promote research, advocacy, social acceptance, and understanding about the disorder of selective mutism. SMF cofounder Sue Newman was instrumental in changing the name of the disorder from elective mutism to selective mutism, as well as updating its diagnostic criteria. Several articles on selective mutism are available at the SMF website.

Selective Mutism Group (SMG)
Childhood Anxiety Network
website: www.selective mutism.org

SMG, part of the Childhood Anxiety Network, is a nonprofit network of families, teachers, psychologists, social workers, speech-language pathologists, and health professionals who are dedicated to increasing public awareness about selective mutism and related childhood anxiety disorders. The SMG advocates for children with selective mutism, promotes research, and provides educational resources about this condition. Its website provides an online library of handouts, resource materials, and articles such as "Silent and Misunderstood" and "Commentary on Cho: Long-Term Effects of Selective Mutism Need Not Be Detrimental."

Stuttering Foundation of America
PO Box 11749,
Memphis, TN 38111-0749
(800) 992-9392
(901) 761-0343
fax: (901) 761-0484
e-mail: info@stuttering help.org
website: www.stuttering help.org

The Stuttering Foundation of America is a nonprofit organization dedicated to providing up-to-date information about the prevention of stuttering in young children and the most effective treatments available for teenagers and adults. The foundation promotes scientific research on stuttering and provides books, DVDs, and brochures on the disorder. An archive of articles, including "Using Brain Imaging to Unravel the Mysteries of Stuttering" and "A Look at Stuttering and Emotions" is available at its website.

FOR FURTHER READING

Books

Victoria Biggs, *Caged in Chaos: A Dyspraxic Guide to Breaking Free.* Philadelphia: Jessica Kingsley, 2005.

Bob B. Bodenhamer, *I Have a Voice: How to Stop Stuttering.* Camarthen, Wales: Crown House, 2011.

Carrie Bryson, *Why Dylan Doesn't Talk: A Real-Life Look at Selective Mutism from the Eyes of a Child.* Lancaster, PA: Sweet Greetings, 2009.

Margaret Fish, *Here's How to Treat Childhood Apraxia of Speech.* San Diego: Plural, 2010.

Malcolm Fraser, *Self-Therapy for the Stutterer.* 11th ed. Memphis: Stuttering Foundation of America, 2010.

Sheila Hale, *The Man Who Lost His Language: A Case of Aphasia.* Philadelphia: Jessica Kingsley, 2007.

Patricia Hamaguchi, *Childhood Speech, Language, and Listening Problems.* 3rd ed. Hoboken, NJ: Wiley, 2010.

Vera Joffe, *Sophie's Story: A Guide to Selective Mutism.* Cambridge: Vera Joffe, 2007.

Mark Logue and Peter Conradi, *The King's Speech: How One Man Saved the British Monarchy.* New York: Sterling, 2010.

Deborah Lott, *Super Star Speech: Speech Therapy Made Simple.* Huntsville, AL: Super Star DML, 2008.

Harianne Mills, *A Mind of My Own: A Memoir of Recovery from Aphasia.* Bloomington, IN: Authorhouse, 2004.

The Stuttering Foundation, *Advice to Those Who Stutter: Expert Help from 28 Therapists Who Stutter Themselves.* 2nd ed. Memphis: Stuttering Foundation of America, 2008.

Periodicals and Internet Sources

Pam Belluch, "A Star Turn for Stuttering, On-Screen and in Research," *New York Times*, February 26, 2011.

Claudia Dunaway, "Using a Counseling Approach When Working with Children with Selective Mutism," California Speech-Language-Hearing Association, Fall 2005. www.csha.org.

Exceptional Parent, "Literacy Program Produces Exciting Results for Children Who Struggle with Speech," September 2009.

Heidi Feldman, "The Purpose of Genetic Testing and Its Relevance to Children with Apraxia," Childhood Apraxia of Speech Association of North America, 2009. www.apraxia-kids.org.

Patti Hamaguchi, "A Case Study of Childhood Apraxia of Speech," Childhood Apraxia of Speech Association of North America, March 22, 2010. www.apraxia-kids.org.

Barry Harbaugh, "A History of Stuttering in the Movies," *Slate*, December 9, 2010. www.slate.com.

Celia Lescano, "Silent Children: Assessment and Treatment of Selective Mutism," *Brown University Child and Adolescent Behavior Newsletter*, January 2008.

Robert T. London, "A Relearning Technique for Stuttering," *Clinical Psychiatry News*, September 2006.

John Mirsky, "Finding My Voice: Love Helps a Stutterer More than Speech Therapy," *Spectator*, January 15, 2011.

William D. Parry, "Reducing Stuttering Blocks by Controlling the Body's Valsalva Mechanism," Valsalva Stuttering Network, June 5, 2011. www.valsalva.org.

Lisa Scott, "Why Speech Therapy?," Stuttering Foundation of America, March 2008. www.stutteringhelp.org.

Nathan Seppa, "Genes May Explain Some Stuttering," *Science News*, March 13, 2010.

Vivian Sisskin, "What Clinicians Can Learn from *The King's Speech*," *Advance: For Speech-Language Pathologists and Audiologists*, 2011.

Stephanie Smith, "Unlocking a Medical Mystery: Stuttering," CNN.com, February 10, 2010. www.cnn.com.

INDEX